THE
HOW TO PULL
COOKBOOK

THE
HOW TO PULL
COOKBOOK

*This book will do for your cooking
what a bottle of merlot will do for your looks!*

Jim Connolly

ODERCIER PRESS

MERCIER PRESS
Douglas Village, Cork, Ireland
www.mercierpress.ie

Trade enquiries to Columba Mercier Distribution,
55a Spruce Avenue, Stillorgan Industrial Park, Blackrock, Dublin

ISBN 1 85635 493 8

10 9 8 7 6 5 4 3 2 1

*Mercier Press receives financial assistance from
the Arts Council/An Chomhairle Ealaíon*

Printed and Bound by J. H. Haynes & Co. Ltd., Sparkford

Contents

Chapter 6 – Sure Bets
Recipes that appear too good for you to have done it yourself

Chapter 7 – Desserts
Guaranteed deal sealers

Chapter 8 – Cocktails
Easy to make – and make him/her easy

Chapter 9 – The Morning After
If things go according to plan you'll need these breakfast recipes which you can whip up in minutes

Acknowledgements

This is harder than it looks. You see if I mention Andrew, I have to mention Pádraig, Joe, Niall and Dara. If I mention Gary and Niamh it means I have to mention John, which means I can't not mention Elaine; and if I've gone that far I might as well as throw Laura, Keelin, Stephanie and Caroline into the pot. Mentioning Steven is a disaster because it'll be which Steven is that – is it the Steven, Peter, Pearl and Frank Steven? Or is it the John and Maura 'I can do impressions' Steven? Similarly, Dave could be the Jarlaith, James, Peter, Jeremy, Philip 'I've got a Royal Flush' Dave or it could be tax planning in several jurisdictions Dave.

All of whom have nowt to do with the book by the way!

On the other hand, Mary, Aisling, Conor and Patrick from Mercier do, so many thanks for delivering a top notch piece of lit.

And finally, thanks to Dave Kenny for encouraging me to shift me arse!

For Jo-Ann

Who'd do anything for a fillet steak

with pepper sauce

Dedications that didn't quite make the cut

For Alex, Shauna and
Bobby
Who'd eat anything
covered in chocolate

For Mum and Dad
Does this cover that loan?

For the lads
Na, Na, Nana, Na

For the chicks who tried,
but failed to nab me
Bet you're sorry you didn't
try harder now

For Jo-Ann
Can I go on that golfing
trip now?

For Demi Moore
I don't suppose I'm on
your list by any chance?

For Elaine, Gary and Steve
Now you have to buy the
book

For Brian Flynn
Sorry, but my parents
might rub this one in a bit

For Gertie
The Nan from Heaven

For Team Taurus
You'll always be Team
SlapUp to me

For Sir Dave Kenny
You gave me a title, so I've
given you one

For Roger
Will you sort out that
artist's exemption now?

For anyone who ate my
rice before I learned
not to stir it
Sorry!

For Mags
My biggest fan

Introduction

You're on the dating circuit. You're a little too old for heavy petting sessions in the parents' house. You've had your fill of al fresco touch-ups and the appeal of a Ford Focus with the seats rolled back has worn off completely. You've moved on. You're now a homeowner and the *modus operandi* of your approach to the opposite sex is maturing. Those classic (and reliable) lines of chat are gone. Never again will you bag another victim with the gem 'finish your drink, you've scored'. No siree. You're now in the zone where statements like 'bring two bottles of wine, an empty stomach and leave your morals at home, you're eating chez moi' roll off your tongue.

And therein lies the problem – he or she's coming to dinner and you've just realised that the bedroom won't be cookin' unless you've baited your prey with a half decent bit of cooking in the kitchen first.

But fear not, dear '*shef*' (when you say it out loud you can't tell the difference, but we know that you're a fraud), that's what we're here for. We are absolutely committed to the illusion of making it appear that you can cook. We really want you to get laid.

And we will succeed in pulling off this scam – guaranteed. How? By following a few simple rules, that's how.

Don't cook if at all possible. If we can get away without actually cooking then that's great – why go for something complicated like deep fried brie when a Caesar salad or prawn cocktail will do the job just as well. (For those of you in the remedial category: you don't have to cook a salad or prawn cocktail.)

We'll only use ingredients that you've actually heard of. You won't find lychees or pancetta in any of our recipes. All of our recipes are made from stuff that'll already be in your cupboard. If they're not in yours they should be in your mother's. Failing this, they will definitely be in your local supermarket.

Educating you on culinary lingo – we'll make you sound like a pro. Even though you won't be using the ingredients you'll be throwing away comments like 'I can't believe that pancetta is so hard to find these days and as for pre-prepared pesto, gimme a break'.

Every recipe has been structured with a super-charged fools guide: *the Remedial Tips*. When we talk about things like say, prawns, we don't assume for a second that you know what we're talking about. So our *remedial guide* tells you what a prawn is, what it looks like and where you find them in the shop.

Our specially selected recipes: ones that make it look like you spent years under Gordon Ramsey's wing, whereas in reality you spent a couple of quid in the supermarket followed by ten minutes cooking. Don't believe us? Then check out what you can do with two eggs, a bowlful of sugar and a block of ice-cream in Chapter 7.

By cheating and taking shortcuts: It's very important to remember that you're not cooking for Delia Smith or

Gary Rhodes. They might be able to spot the difference between homemade and frozen garlic bread but the person at your table won't. So the rule of thumb is: if you won't get the credit for making it yourself, don't bother – buy it instead.

And finally, you should feel reassured by the fact that all of these recipes have been used countless times by the author – someone who never got paid to cook, a regular Joe just like you.

So *shef*, we wish you well. Go forth and cook. Fingers crossed you'll impress your guest enough that chapter 9 will actually be used. If you do happen to score, the author would appreciate photographic evidence, for, eh … research purposes, em, yes, research purposes.

Bon appetite!
(French term wishing you a 'Good Appetite' for your meal. And if you actually didn't know this you really do have the right book in your hands.)

CHAPTER 1

THE *VERY* BASICS

Your Cooker

One of the absolutely fundamental things to understand is that you are not the only one who doesn't know how your cooker works – neither do we. Number 3 on Jeremy's eight-ring aga probably feels an awful lot hotter then Number 3 on Tina's two-ring camping stove but who knows?

COOKER LEVEL	WHAT WILL HAPPEN TO A SAUCEPAN OF BOILING WATER WHEN LEFT ON THE RING
Full Blast *That's number 5 on a knob that goes up to number 5*	*It will bubble like a turbo charged Jacuzzi*
Medium *Number 3 on the five-knob scale*	*Normal Jacuzzi-like bubbling*
Low *Just turn the knob to the first notch*	*Imagine a Jacuzzi powered by farts alone*

The point is that it's really very very important that you know the difference between these temperatures on YOUR cooker. Similarly, you need to pay some attention to your grill. Check out how long it takes to toast some bread – milliseconds on Full Blast and just far too long on Low. How many times have you stuck a nice Gino Ginelli in the grill on max power? You stick it in upside down to get a nice bit of action going on the pizza bread (only takes a couple of minutes at which stage the grill is really firing out the rays). You flip it over and the cheese melts and burns in moments while the middle of the pizza is still frozen solid.

Yep – if you pay your grill a little bit of attention, she'll repay you in spades.

And we mean this. Don't you dare try one of our recipes on some mank-ridden grill tray. Your grill will repay you with a lovely black gritted look on your steak and do its best to treat you to a nice bit of gastroenteritis at the same time. Your grill will do its best to prevent you from scoring with anyone else until you show it a bit of attention first.

Measurements

When you are in the middle of making some Michelin Three-Star pastry dish, the smallest deviation from the recipe may be crucial. In this book it doesn't really matter. If the recipe calls for two tomatoes and you only have one, so what? What's the worst that can happen? If you're supposed to add a quarter pint of wine and somehow a ½ pint falls in – so what? It's highly unlikely that small changes to the recipe are going to make any real difference to the final dish. So don't be uptight about your measurements – consider all of the measurements contained in the ingredients as approximations, the same way that most blokes claim to possess equipment that is *approximately* six inches. When it transpires that there's only a fraction available for delivery, you still end up with something enjoyable (at least she'll say it was enjoyable!). Similarly, the ladies always claim to be *approximately* 8 stone – yeah right!

Tricks of the Trade

Cooking is just one element of a successful fed and bed exercise. The following tricks of the trade will enhance your chances of actually meaning it when you ask how they like their eggs in the morning.

You've heard of the 'looks aren't everything' saying? Well when you're entertaining, the motto is 'cooking isn't everything either'. A crap meal served on a chipped plate will leave a far worse impression than a crap meal served on a lovely piece of Denby. Similarly, a good bottle of wine will mask serious imperfections in your cooking.

So basically you should aim to take as much emphasis away from the cooking as possible.

There are three areas that you'll need to pay attention to:

Lighting

Badly cooked meals look far more appetising when you can't really make them out. Candlelight works a treat. And all this time you thought it was a romantic gesture – no worries, your guest will still think it is.

Wine

Basic rules of cooking would suggest that you serve red wine with red meat dishes and white wine with chicken or fish dishes. You can cut out all of that political correctness and make yourself out to be a wine connoisseur by inserting the name of the wine and the name of your meal in the following statement (which you will make while opening the bottle):

'They say that some wines are not appropriate with [*name of dish*] but I just find that a nice bottle of [*name of wine*] really sets off the innate flavourings of this meal.'

Now just keep pouring – no matter how bad the wine is, it will taste like nectar after the second bottle.

Music

FOR BLOKES ENTERTAINING GIRLS	FOR GIRLS ENTERTAINING BLOKES	SUITABLE FOR EITHER
Soundtrack to any chick-flick: *Scent of a Woman, Titanic, etc.*	Soundtrack to any Quentin Tarantino movie: *Pulp Fiction, Kill Bill, Reservoir Dogs;* or any Barry White CD	Any 'Best of' albums: ELO, *Squeeze Abba*
DEFINITE NO NOS	NO NOS	NO NOS
Barry White – you might as well put a condom on the side plate	Brittany Spears – face it, no matter how good-looking you are you won't be as good-looking as our Brittany, so best not remind him	*Best of Coldplay –* you won't sleep together but you will sleep!

CHAPTER 2

FOUR PLAY

Starters that use only four ingredients

Melony Prawn Cocktail
Smoked Salmon Wraps
Bruschetta
Homemade Tortilla Chips
with Tomato Salsa

Melony Prawn Cocktail

INGREDIENTS

How much	Of what	Where to find them
1	melon	Somewhere near the apples
200g	tiger prawns	Depends on how much you want to spend – frozen prawns will be somewhere near the fish fingers, whereas fresh prawns will be at the fresh meat/fish counter
3 tbsp (heaped)	mayonnaise	In your/your mother's fridge
1 tbsp (heaped)	ketchup	Oh come on

If you happen to have any 1980s cookery programmes video-taped, you're bound to see the prawn cocktail featured. We've updated this classic simple starter by replacing the bed of lettuce – that would have appeared in the 1980s cookery show – with melon. Simple yet inspired. Your guest will be thinking one of two things:

A.   God the prawns and Marie Rose sauce are so nostalgic yet the melon is so bold and daring – I'm going to sleep with this cook before dessert.

B.   Oh, fish, fruit and pink stuff – pass me the wine.

You'll win either way.

Remedial Tips

Prawns are a shellfish that look something like Sigourney Weaver's Alien, but much smaller. You can buy them fresh but then you'll have to take some sort of evening class to find out how to release the meaty innards from the armoured shell and then you'll have the further complication of having to cook the little buggers.

Alternatively you can buy them shelled and cooked. At this stage they look like the pinky/orangey things you find in your prawn curry.

Shelled and cooked prawns can be bought frozen or fresh and they come in different sizes – tiger prawns typically being the biggest (about the size of your little finger). Very few eaters can tell the difference between a once frozen prawn and a fresh one, so base your purchase on your estimate of your guests eating skills! If in doubt, go for the fresh ones.

Where Most People go Wrong
It's very hard to make a balls of this dish but there are two common mistakes:

1. Buying a melon that's too hard – the easiest way to make sure that you buy a nice ripe melon is to ASK. If you are to believe any of the supermarket ads these days, not only will you get the perfect melon but you're also likely to get a ten minute lecture on how to serve it.

2. Not drying the prawns – if you've decided on the tight-arse approach to the meal, you'll start with a frozen block of ice and prawns. These need to defrost fully by placing them in a sieve so that the excess fluid runs off. Then you should rinse them in fresh water and leave them to drain. Now pat them dry with some kitchen towel. If you don't, the excess liquid will turn your Marie Rose sauce into a runny mess.

The Recipe
• Prepare the prawns, as above.

• Ball the melon – for those in the Montessori class this means that you scoop out little balls of melon using an implement known as a melon-baller. If you can't lay your hands on one of these, do your best to chop the melon into little blocks (dice the bugger).

• Mix the mayonnaise and the ketchup in a cup – you should end up with pink mayonnaise. Go on, dip your finger in and taste it – nice eh! You now have a Marie Rose sauce.

Well done, that's the cooking finished. All you need to do now is serve it as follows:

- Place a bed of melon balls on a suitable plate or glass bowl (about 4 tablespoons of them)
- Place half of the prawns on top (neatly there, *shef*)
- Spoon 1–2 tablespoons of the Marie Rose sauce on top of the prawns (try not to get any on the melon).

Oh yeah baby, you're cooking now.

Smoked Salmon Wraps

INGREDIENTS

How much	Of what	Where to find them
4	tortilla wraps	For some reason all the food of foreign origin is stacked together, so check near the rice and the pasta
1 small tub	cream cheese	In Philadelphia
1 pack (100g)	smoked salmon	Depending on the size of the shop they'll either be beside the milk and cheese or in front of the guy with the red and white stripy apron
1	lemon	Pre-cut versions are available behind the local bar

Ah yes, this is what this book is all about – not cooking if at all possible. To your guest, this starter says so much about you as a cook. It says that you're fresh. It says that you're creative and experimental. It says that you're sophisticated yet primitive. It basically says that you're good marriage material.

Only you know that it really should say that you're simple, lazy and cheap but if they buy all the other bullshit who cares? Your dinner guest will be looking to read between the lines at all stages of the night and as soon as they clap eyes on this dish they'll be thinking:

A. Salmon? Is there something fishy about me or is it that I'm a wise catch?

B. Wraps? Is the relationship to be kept under wraps or do they want to wrap me up?

Look, you're already in control and you haven't even had to get them drunk first.

Remedial Tips

Salmon is pronounced *Sammon* not *Sall-man*. Salmon (fish by the way) break their nuts to swim back to the very place they were born to have their own kids. Aaahh. As well as overcoming grizzly bears, raging rapids and unimaginable terrain, the old salmon also gets shafted by fishermen who like to catch them, hang them in an outhouse and light fires nearby to infuse them with a smokey flavour. Make sure that your guest appreciates the great lengths you and the salmon have gone to to feed them. The least you deserve is a bit of first base action.

Where Most People go Wrong

Seriously, you cannot go wrong here. This is because there is no cooking involved. It's a mere assembly process. If you do go wrong, you're probably daft and you've gone and bought a tin of salmon instead of the nice sliced pieces that you need for this dish. If you have done this and you don't have time to replace it you'll have to improvise and use the tin. Don't you dare tell your guest that it was one of my recipes though — I've a reputation to protect. If they happen to really like your version, you can ignore the last sentence.

The Recipe

OK, this should only take a minute! Basically what we're doing here is making a posh sandwich thing:

- Start by spreading some of the cheese on each of the wraps.
- Next place a slice of the salmon on top.
- Squeeze some lemon juice on top of that, and sprinkle some salt and black pepper on top of that.

That's it, cooking complete!

Now roll up the wrap like a swiss-roll and cut off the ends to make it more presentable. Two each will do the job. Don't forget to tell Sammy Salmon's life story so that you can cash in on the first base entitlement!

Bruschetta

INGREDIENTS

How much	Of what	Where to find them
3	vine tomatoes	Put that can down and go back to the fruit and veg section
2	garlic cloves	Beside the crucifixes, the silver bullets and the wooden stakes in the vampire section
1	french stick	In the bakery section – an XL baguette, basically
2 tbsp	olive oil	If it's not already in your press go to the freezer door and stick your tongue to it as punishment, fool

Here's how to really impress your guest.

When they walk in, tell them what you're having for a main course and then pretend that you've completely and utterly forgotten to pick up the ingredients for the starter. So, looking a little flustered, you go to the fridge and start humming and hawing as if you're trying to concoct something really quickly out of a few basic ingredients – tomatoes, bread, garlic – and then snap your fingers saying, 'sure we'll have some "broos-ketta"' (that's the correct pronunciation).

Men will benefit from this approach as it just makes them look so creative, spontaneous and worldly. The fact that you had forgotten the ingredients for the original starter will be perceived as sweet, even quaint, in an 'ahhh, isn't he sweet, forgetting the ingredients; sure he's all nervous, poor lamb' kind of way.

Women will benefit from this approach because it says 'look, I'm fantastic in the kitchen' whilst the other message about the forgotten ingredients says 'you're not that impor-tant to me yet luv' – the casual approach, and oh, how a man loves a chase.

Remedial Tips

Tomatoes are fantastic. You'll recognise them as the red bits in your BLT. What you probably didn't know is that they're classed as a fruit. Apparently this is because their seeds are on the inside, like all other fruit. Whoever came up with this must have forgotten about the auld strawberry!

Peeling a tomato is usually a pointless exercise except for dishes like this. And here's the way to do it: boil some wa-ter; drop in your tomatoes; wait for about 2 minutes; take them out. Now an old housewives' tale is that if the skin falls away easily, then your lover's clothes will do the same thing that very night. If the skin is no easier to get off than a normal tomato, you're going to have to rip off your lover's clothes, or does it mean that you should dunk your lover in water – ah it's something like that.

Where Most People go Wrong

You have to toast the bread under a grill. You will burn the bread unless you stand by your grill, whipping it in and out every ten seconds. Only leave your station if you hear those immortal words: 'I'm going upstairs to slip into something more comfortable.'

The Recipe

There are two stages to this meal: the toasting of the bread and the preparation of the stuff to put on top. You need to prepare the topping first.

- First, peel your tomatoes, per the *Remedial Tip*.

- Now chop them as finely as you can but try to leave the seeds and watery bits behind.

- Dump them into a glass bowl (use a clean one as you'll be serving it up in this).

- Now chop up one of the garlic cloves as finely as you can and add it to the tomatoes.

- Add a tablespoon of olive oil, some salt and pepper and stir it around.

Now, when it's coming close to the time you want to serve the starter you should fire up the grill to about 3 or 4 on the five-notch scale.

- Cut the baguette into thick slices and try to cut the bread diagonally – this gives you more surface area of bread.

- Next toast one side of the bread.

- Remove it and drizzle olive oil on the raw side. Try to drizzle it evenly over as much of the area as you can without drowning the slice.

- Now peel the remaining garlic clove, rub it all over the oil-covered side of each slice, and return them for toasting.

- Once nicely browned, remove them. Be careful here because the oil covered bits won't brown half as quickly as the bits you missed.

Now there are two ways to move on from here:

- You could dump some of the mixture on top and put it back under the grill and serve up the bruschetta in a pizza-like fashion.

- Alternatively you could simply serve up the toast and let guests top it themselves.

Naturally, option two is less risky so I'd go for that one. Anyway you've done enough, take a load off and enjoy the approval, or the chase, depending on your gender!

Homemade Tortilla Chips with Tomato Salsa

INGREDIENTS

How much	Of what	Where to find them
3	vine tomatoes	Any would-be drug dealer will have a greenhouse full of these to camouflage the hemp plants, seriously!
2	garlic cloves	They actually come in bulbs – should be near the onions
1 tbsp	olive oil	In your press
2	tortilla wraps	Look for any Mexicans in the shop, and follow them

I still impress myself with this fraudulence. And your date will be equally as impressed. As a result of serving this starter, I guarantee you that at some stage during the evening you'll be hit with the old onion analogy: 'My God, you've got so many layers, a great cook, great conversationalist, great taste in dates (tee-hee), you're like an onion – the more I peel away, the more layers I find.' At this stage you know you're in but there are two ways to play it depending on your gender:

Things appropriate for a woman to say in response:
Blokes are fairly shallow and really just want some action, so the following line will work wonders:

'Yes I may be an onion emotionally, but clothes-wise I'm more like an orange, one layer and you're sinking your teeth into flesh.'

(If you want, you can rip off some clothes to emphasise the point, as blokes can also be a bit slow on the uptake.)

Things appropriate for a bloke to say in response:
Girls are looking for something deep if they come out with this rubbish in the first place so don't say 'sorry, I missed that. Did you say something about onions? It's just that I got distracted by your cleavage'. No, something more along the lines of the following will be more appropriate:

'Yes, most people think of me as an onion, whereas I think of myself as an iceberg onion – only one third of my layers will be seen by anyone – you'll need to know me a lot better to go deeper.'

Watch her swoon; I think you may just have clinched it.

Remedial Tips
Tortillas are Mexican flatbreads made from cornflour. It never struck me that a tortilla wrap and a tortilla chip are related. But they are. They're not just related; they're the same bloody thing. If you cut your tortilla wrap into wedge shapes, and fry them – ta-daaa, you get tortilla chips. Your

onion-like aura has just sprouted an extra layer for your date to peel off. They will be so impressed with this trivia when you drop it into the conversation.

Where Most People go Wrong
Overdoing the chips is where you'll go wrong and if you don't get that wrong, you'll forget to drain the excess oil from them when they're done. Pay attention to these two issues and you're sorted.

The Recipe
You'll notice a certain laziness to my cooking the further you get into this book, but here's where the laziness starts:

- You see the last recipe – Bruschetta? You see that whole section on how to prepare the topping? Great, because another name for that topping is Tomato Salsa. Off you go now and follow that recipe and come back to this one when you're ready.

Next step is to deep fry the tortilla:

- Cut the flat bread into wedge-shaped slices – you should be familiar with the size to aim for.
- Fire up the deep fat fryer to 190°C and pop in the tortilla wedges, about ten at a time.
- Leave them in for about 3–4 minutes, remove and dry them off using kitchen towel.
- Do the same for the rest of the wedges.

Now serve them up together – not bad eh, amigo?

CHAPTER 3

BITS ON THE SIDE

Rice
Pasta
Potatoes
Vegetables

Most cookbooks take it for granted that you know how to boil a potato. Not this one! We know that, although you may be very good at ordering sauté mushrooms and creamed potatoes, you wouldn't know how to cook them if your life depended on it. Allow me to enlighten you …

Rice

INGREDIENTS

How much	Of what	Where to find them?
1½ pint	long grain rice	For some reason they're always in the same aisle as the beans
1 pint	vegetable stock	Use a stock cube – you'll find one in your or your neighbour's press
5 strands	saffron	Don't bother even looking, just ask

Most people who give up cooking usually do so after cooking rice. They just can't understand why their rice always turns out like the squidgy, mushy slop your dad always dished up when your mother was sick.

Only one thing differentiates lovely fluffy boiled rice – à la the local take-away – from the stodgy swill you've made a hundred times. And that is a spoon – you cock rice up by stirring it. Stirring rice breaks the grain and releases all of the starch thus transforming it into prison food instantaneously. So, what have we learned? DON'T STIR THE RICE. Have you ever wondered why the boil in the bag stuff always turns out better? Yep – you can't stir it when it's in the bag. Bet you feel silly paying all that extra money now. Once you've mastered cooking rice my way your date will voice their approval with some blatant come on such as 'oooh! That rice was sooo good – if it was on a take-away menu it would be item 69'.

Remedial Tips

Rice comes in various forms – Basmati, Brown Rice, Risotto Rice, etc. Anything other than long grain rice is for the university standard cooks. You are in the montessori class – start with the long grain rice first and get that right before asking questions about other types.

Rice absorbs almost exactly twice its volume of water before it's cooked, so if you want more rice, simply increase the measures proportionately – 1 pint rice, 2 pints of liquid, etc.

Rice cooks in about 12 minutes but you should always taste it to make sure. After a while you'll know simply by looking but until then simply taste.

People who know a lot about eating usually know bugger all about cooking but rest assured they are the ones who will talk about the tenderness of the rice. Basically these people are tossers but they speaketh the truth. Perfectly cooked rice should be firm, not soft like a marshmallow. Personally, I couldn't care either way once you haven't stirred the stuff.

Saffron is a spice that adds flavour but also turns the rice yellow. Very aesthetically pleasing, but optional nonetheless. See Remedial Tip on page 81.

Where Most People go Wrong

Four things can go pear-shaped on you when it comes to cooking rice:

1. Under-cooking it – tastes like you're eating wood splinters. This won't happen if you taste it during cooking.
2. Really over-cooking it – you can get away with a bit of over-cooking where the rice takes on the marshmallow quality mentioned above. But if you don't stop cooking it at this stage your rice will arrive at the 'looks like a bowl of porridge' stage in about 2 minutes. Of course if you pay attention to the 12 minute cooking time, this won't happen.
3. Not using enough stock – basically the rice absorbs all the liquid and then begins to spontaneously combust.
4. Stirring the rice – do I have to say it again?

The Recipe

Ready? Here we go. To make 1 pint of rice, which will be enough for two servings:

• Bring the stock to the boil (and by the way, to make the stock, boil the pint of water and crumble the stock cube into it).

• Carefully add the rice to the boiling stock.

• Crumble in the saffron strands (optional).

• Turn down the cooker and simmer for 12 minutes. Remember to taste it before you take it off the cooker to make sure it's done.

• Drain the rice in a sieve and serve.

Well done. If you had a fortune cookie it would probably say 'stick on the Barry White CD, you're in'.

Pasta

INGREDIENTS

How much	Of what	Where to find them
2 portions	pasta	Somewhere near the Pot Noodles
2 pints	vegetable stock	The trusted stock cubes will do nicely – check your press, in behind the teabags

Tagliatelle, Radiatori, Spaghetti, Macaroni, LoadaBoloney, the list is endless. Most people think that there are only five or six pasta variations, similar to the way that most Italians only think that there is one way to serve a potato (by chipping them – when was the last time you were in an Italian restaurant and got offered potatoes any other way!). The reality however is that there are in excess of 150 types of pasta and the list grows every time that a chef or manufacturer thinks of a new shape to use.

The fundamental thing to know about pasta is that, apart from the shape, they are all made from the same thing: wheat and water – that's it. Any of the dried pasta that you'll be using in these recipes comes in a packet and if you check out the ingredients on the side, it'll most likely say '100% Durum Wheat', nothing else. So if it's Penne, Spaghetti or whatever, the only difference is the shape of the pasta. Amazing, isn't it!

There are, of course, exceptions to this rule, the obvious ones being the green pasta that you'll notice on the shelf – Pasta Verde, as the locals would call it. These are pasta shapes that have had spinach worked into the dough. Another variation is Pasta al Uovo – pasta made with eggs as well as the wheat. Despite these minor complications, the beauty of pasta is that no matter what shaped pasta you have in your mitt, they are all cooked exactly the same way; so once you know how to cook spaghetti, you also know how to cook all of the other variations.

And this is where the descriptions set out in the *remedial tips* will come in handy, because there is nothing sexier than a well-informed and knowledgeable dinner host who knows how to distinguish one pasta from another. Your guest will be left in awe. This skill will follow you around forever because rest assured, the next time you're out for a meal, someone will ask: what's Fusilli like? Now you know how daft a question that really is. 'It's like any other pasta, Dopey, but it's shaped like a spiral', but I'm sure you'll manage to put it more diplomatically.

Remedial Tips
The only pasta shapes you're likely to encounter in an Italian restaurant based anywhere other than Italy are:

Name	Pronunciation	What it looks like	How much to use
Spaghetti	Spa-gety	Spaghetti	For each portion use about as much spaghetti as would fit down the neck of a coke bottle
Conchiglie	Conch-igly	Shells	Use a good handful for each portion
Farfalle	Far-faly	Bow-ties	Use a good handful for each portion
Fusilli	Fuz-ili	Spirals	Use a good handful for each portion
Linguine	Lin-gweeny	Flat spaghetti	Measure the same way as spaghetti
Penne	Pen-eh	Tubes	Use a good handful for each portion
Macaroni	Macker-own-y	Semi-circular tubes	Use a good handful for each portion
Ravioli	Rav-e-o-lee	Pillows	See directions on pack
Tagliatelle	Tag-lee-a-telly	Flat ribbons	Usually comes in nests – use 2/3 nests per person

Where Most People go Wrong

Over-cooking pasta is really the only way to go wrong. And if it is over-cooked, it's usually fairly obvious! The pasta shaped like penne won't have any structure left – the tubes will collapse into a sorry looking pile of sludge. Although it won't kill you, you'll find this very hard to stomach because it's just so slimy. The remedy – bin them and start again, which will only cost you about 8 minutes.

Ideally pasta should still be firm to the bite. In pretentious conversation you should refer to the firmness as 'al dente', which basically means 'it's got bite' in Italian.

The Recipe
Are we ready? Decided on your pasta? Let's go so …

This really is simplicity itself.

- Start by bringing the stock to the boil and make sure the water is bubbling like a Jacuzzi that's just had a nitrous oxide boost.

- Add your pasta; give it a quick stir to make sure none has stuck to the bottom of the saucepan.

- Walk away and come back in about 7 minutes to test the product. It should be almost ready at this stage – still firm but very easy to bite through. If it's still crunchy leave it for another minute or two and take some codeine for the broken teeth.

- When ready, pour the pasta into a sieve or colander. You can keep the pasta warm by leaving the colander sit over some simmering water until you're ready to serve it up.

That's it. Now you know why most Italians claim to be great cooks – there's nothing to it. No wonder they've such a romantic reputation – of the two hours it takes to serve you a meal they've only been cooking for about 10 minutes – the rest of the time they've been smoozing you!

Potatoes

Ah yes. There's very little an Oirishman can't tell you about the humble spud. It used to be the subject of one of the most popular chat-up lines for blokes in the late 1800s and early 1900s: 'So Mary, tell me, how would ya be cookin' me tate-ahs now for me dinner then?' If Mary was able to give the right answer then she was made for life – a dirty great Irish farmer and ten of his offspring as a prize. Ironically, in many cases, pissed-off Marys poisoned their fellas with the potato. You see, the potato comes from the Nightshade family (poisonous plants in case it's news to you) and the leaves of the plant are poisonous. I'm telling ya. You'll never see a cow tucking into a potato plant and that's why farmers can grow potatoes beside grazing cattle. You won't see him doing the same with a field of carrots!

Don't you just love the subject of potatoes already? And I'm only getting warmed up. Did you know that spuds were originally introduced to Europe about 500 years ago by Spaniards returning from Peru. Your mates will be very impressed when you blurt that fact out nonchalantly over a few glasses of vino in the beer garden.

So basically we've been stuffing ourselves with spuds for 500 years and there's very little we haven't done to them yet. We've boiled them, steamed, baked, mashed, sautéed and waffled them. But the award for the 'what will we do to the potato next' competition goes to whoever thought of chippin' them. So we'll start there first.

Chips

Aka Pommes Frites
Aka French Fries

INGREDIENTS

How much	Of what	Where to find them
3	potatoes (tennis ball sized)	Probably in the press under the sink in your mum's house

Ah, the memories. Heading into Liberos after a couple of shandies on a Friday night and shouting from the back of the queue: 'All right there Libero – any chips left?' 'Course we got chips left stupido.' 'Serves ya right for making too many so!'

It's a fact that no matter how hard you try, you'll never make chips at home that taste as nice as the ones from the take-away. There are a few trains of thought as to what the difference might be attributable. Top of the list is salt – you never put on as much salt on the homemade ones as the bloke does with the ones in the take-away. Second is vinegar, for the same reasons. Third is the stuff that the chips are cooked in. Yours will be cooked in nice fresh vegetable oil whereas the ones from the chipper are cooked in lard (animal fat). If that's not bad enough the ones that aren't sold are reheated by dunking them in more hot animal fat. This ensures that they taste spectacular whilst hardening your arteries at the same time.

Remedial Tips

Unfortunately potatoes have to be peeled before you chip them. This means removing all of the skin. This includes those awkward little eyes. So don't be lazy – do a proper job.

The trick to impressing your date with a chip is to take the peeled spud and square it off. This means cutting off the bumpy edges so that you're left with a nice symmetrical rectangle-shaped potato. Now, simply take your time and cut the rectangle into identically sized chips. You don't want long skinny ones, you should be aiming for chips that are about the same thickness as a Twix finger, and half as long. About twelve of these per serving will do the job nicely.

Where Most People go Wrong

When you've finished chipping your spuds you need to keep them in water until you're ready to cook them. If you don't they go brown. They won't kill you or do you any harm, they just look gank. When the cooking time comes it's vitally important to dry off the chips before plonking them in the hot oil. As you know, oil and water don't mix and sticking a wet chip into boiling oil will cause the skin of the chip to be nuked. It will still be edible but it just won't be take-away standard. So get some kitchen towel and dry your chips before cooking them.

The Recipe

Ready? Fire up the deep fat fryer and let's go. There is nothing to this.

- Your deep fat fryer will probably have a dial with a picture of a few chips on it. If it doesn't, turn it to 180°C.

- Add the chips to the basket and when the light goes out lower the basket and leave them for 3 minutes. Then give the basket a quick shake to make sure the ones that got stuck together are freed up to get a nice all round tan.

- After a further 5 to 6 minutes turn the fryer up to 190°C and cook the chips until they look like they've spent a week in the canaries.

- The trick is to tip them onto kitchen towel to dry off the excess grease. Now sprinkle salt over them – by the time your date sprinkles their own usual amount of salt on the chips, we'll be up to the excessive levels that the guys in the take-away use.

Finally, when you're presenting the plate of whatever and chips, take a bit of time to arrange the lovely symmetrical chips into some form of Lego-like structure. Try to make it into a bed shape and plant some Freudian messages that your date won't realise consciously. As they're licking the salt off their lips after they're finished, they'll probably say something extremely flirtatious like 'I'm so sated by those chips I could sleep right now'. If this happens, strike while the iron's hot.

Boiled Potatoes

INGREDIENTS

How much	Of what	Where to find them
4	potatoes (tennis ball sized)	Fresh ones can be stolen from most elderly neighbours' gardens

Now there's a clue in the name here as to the process one might use to cook a boiled potato. If you haven't guessed yet then you are the very market that this book is aimed at. Boy are you getting value for money. In case the hamster is still working it out, boiled potatoes are cooked by boiling them (in water). I could stop here but I really want to make sure you don't muck this up, as the boiled spud is the building block for the next few recipes.

Remedial Tips

When it comes to boiling potatoes, you really need some expert guidance on the type of potato to use. Contrary to what you might think, all spuds do not have the same properties. Some maintain a very firm shape when boiled and some self-destruct and turn into sludge. Depending on which supermarket you use, you'll probably be confronted with half a dozen choices of potato so it's safest to ask which is best for boiling. If you intend acquiring the merchandise Batman style by robin' them, you may wish to enquire from the neighbours first.

A handy tip for presenting a boiled potato is to be different. You've probably eaten them a thousand times but have you ever had a rectangular block of boiled loveliness served up to you before? Seriously, it's all in the presentation. Once you've finished peeling the potatoes, cut off the edges so that you're left with a nice big chunky block of potato. Even if they're overcooked and served with the most horrible main course, they'll still be a talking point. You'll become known as the one with the square spuds.

Where Most People go Wrong

The length of time it takes to boil a potato depends wholly on their size. Most people go wrong by over cooking them at which stage they disintegrate and turn into soup.

The Recipe

Ready? The suspense must be killing you so let me reveal how we boil a potato:

- Put the peeled spuds into a pot of cold water, and turn the ring on to full blast.

- When the water reaches turbo Jacuzzi mode, flick the knob to medium.

- Wait about ten minutes and check for doneness by stabbing the potato with a sharp knife. You should continue to check every two minutes until the potato takes on a Danish pastry-like resistance to the blade.

- Drain all of the water and you're ready to go.

Congratulations. You can now move on to the senior infants class for the next few recipes.

Sautéed Potatoes

(posh chips basically)

INGREDIENTS

How much	Of what	Where to find them
4	boiled potatoes	Wherever you left them to cool

How to piss off a posh restaurateur, lesson no. 1: Ask how small the 'minute' steak is and then ask for chips with it.

It's a fact of restaurant life. Some places have egos that preclude them from serving chips. That doesn't, however, stop restaurant goers from wanting them. So as a sort of compromise, sauté potatoes were invented – a sort of hybrid between a boiled potato and a chip. I haven't actually tested this but I reckon that the auld sauté spud could actually be worse for you than the chip, but the good news is that they taste better so you can justify the fact that your coronary arteries will harden a little quicker.

Remedial Tips

The word 'sauté' comes from the French for 'jump'. 'Sauté Jacques sur Jill', for example. If you've ever seen those cookery programmes where the chef is tossing stuff in a frying pan, the likelihood is that he is sautéing something. However, for the purpose of this dish let's assume that sautéing simply means frying in a little hot fat. When the precious little slices of potato need to be turned don't try to toss them à la Jamie Oliver – they'll end up on the floor, under the microwave or they'll stick to the expelair. Simply turn them carefully with a knife or whatever. They'll still end up as sautés – they just won't have been sautéed, capiche?

The second trick of the trade concerns the substance that you use to fry them in. A little vegetable oil or olive oil will do the trick just nicely but for a real 'oh my God, how did you make those posh chips' reaction, you should use a little quality fat. You see the potatoes will suck up all of the grease in the pan and assume the associated flavour. The more savoury the grease the more unhealthy and the more tasty the result. Personally I find frying a couple of juicy sausages and streaky rashers first will leave a nice greasy pan behind. Sautés cooked in this stuff spell quality. This attention to detail could mark the difference between lips and tongues later.

Where Most People go Wrong

Two things catch people out with these babies:

1. First is the temptation to sauté them properly by tossing them, thus losing half of the portion to the floor.

2. The second is to cook them at the wrong temperature – too hot and they'll burn, too cool and they'll soak up the grease without crisping up. The trick is to make sure the oil/fat is already at a medium heat before placing the potatoes on the pan.

Ready? Alez nouz, so (as they say in a pidgin-French speaking type country).

The Recipe

- Cut the boiled potato into uniform slices – about the thickness of a digestive biscuit.

- Heat the pan as described above in point two and fry the potato slices for about 4 minutes each side.

- Don't constantly poke and prod them – leave them alone. Most people associate cooking with constant stirring, touching, tossing, turning, etc. It makes them feel better to be doing something. Trust me, walk away and come back in 4 minutes, they won't be burnt (unless you missed the instruction to turn the knob to medium). When you turn them they should have a nice crisp golden colour. Do the same on the other side and you're done.

- Dry them off with a little kitchen towel and sprinkle a little salt over them.

Sit back and pucker up for that lippy kiss that's already 50% guaranteed.

Mashed (Creamed) Potatoes

INGREDIENTS

How much	Of what	Where to find them
4	boiled potatoes	In the saucepan on the cooker
1	knob of butter	Fridge (anyone's)
Some	milk	As above
Some	salt and pepper	In small jars with the letters 'S' and 'P' dotted on the top

Mashed potatoes probably represent the foodstuff that you've eaten most frequently in your life. You love them, but the funny thing is that although you may love your mummy's creamed spuds, that's no guarantee that you'll like all versions. You see, we have definitely hit on the recipe that splits most wannabe and real cooks – how to mash a spud. Really, there is no textbook way how to do it. Even the ingredients vary. In addition to the ones I use below others include cream, cheese, onion, hot milk and beaten eggs.

But they're all wrong. Anyone who mashes potatoes in any other way to that identified below is a pretentious fraud. Milk, butter, salt and pepper, end of story. Just ask my mum, so there.

And for the special tip that will ensure your girlfriend or boyfriend gets really impressed, it is vitally important to note the serving trick. You see, a well mashed spud has characteristics and properties similar to plaster – it can be smoothed out using a wet knife – no kidding. So the idea is to place a dollop of mash on the plate and mould it into a relevant shape – a love heart for example. This gives the end product an almost artificial appearance – it's that good looking. Your date will take one look at their plate and immediately think:

Her: 'Awwww, a love heart, he's trying to tell me he's all mushy inside.'

Him: 'Ah, Jeasus look – a love heart – the way to a man's stomach is to serve up a hearty meal.'

Remedial Tips

You have to mash potatoes immediately after they have finished boiling. You can't take a two-day old boiled spud from the fridge, zap it in the microwave and then mash it – it just won't work. You have to mash them on the spot. This means that you have to pay a bit more attention to your cooking times when serving creamed potatoes. But there's no need to be obsessive as mash potatoes also have another quite astounding property – they are better insulators than a lagging jacket, which means that they'll stay surprisingly hot for a long time – I'm talking tens of minutes here, not hours. Taste them before serving – if they've gone cold, pay special heed to the next paragraph.

Where Most People go Wrong

The one thing about creamed potatoes is that it can be difficult to reheat them using anything other than a microwave. This is because they burn really easily in a saucepan. And when they burn they produce an odour that would put bean-based flatulence in the shade. The smell of burnt potatoes has the same uniqueness that burnt toast has – you'll always know what has burned simply by the smell. But what's worse about potatoes is that the smell permeates the whole saucepan full of mash, rendering them inedible – well edible but disgusting.

The Recipe

Lets grab your masher and do it so.

• First thing to do with your pot of freshly boiled spuds is to drain every bit of water from them. Failure to do so will make them unnecessarily soggy.

• In the same pot, mash the spuds as well as possible.

• Now put in a good knob of butter – the amount really depends on your own preference. If you're unsure, put in about a teaspoonful.

• Also put in some salt and pepper – a good bit of salt but lots of pepper always yields a good result.

• Continue mashing – the spuds will probably appear quite dry still but will start to bind together.

- Finally add the milk. Again, the amount you use depends on your own taste. The more milk you use, the creamier (or mushier) your spuds will become. I tend to err on the lesser side so that the finished product is still quite firm. This makes the moulding process described above easier to achieve.

Baked Potato

INGREDIENTS

How much	Of what	Where to find them
4	potatoes (tennis ball sized)	On the stage after a Coldplay concert (also a good place to find tomatoes and eggs)
1	sheet of tinfoil	Unwrap the sandwiches that your mum gave you when you left home and use that foil

This is definitely the laziest and most foolproof way to cook a spud. If you think you might get lucky before dinner these are definitely the potatoes to go for because these babies will survive hours of overcooking.

Remedial Tips

Baking a potato is nowhere near as arduous as, say, baking a cake. You do need an oven but that's where the similarities end. The term 'baking' is a bit misleading in this instance because it suggests some form of cooking. As you'll see from the instructions below, nothing could be further from the truth.

Where Most People go Wrong

There really is only one way to go wrong and that is to undercook the spud. Your guest will break their wrist and their knife trying to cut it and even after all the hard work, the slice that they've excavated will be inedible.

The Recipe

Ready for the quickest lesson yet?

- Fire up the oven to about 180°C.

- Start by washing the potatoes – wash 'em well because most people eat the skins.

- Prick them with a fork.

- Wrap them in tinfoil – (individually, not together!)

- Bung them in the oven for anywhere from 50 minutes to 4 hours! They'll be perfect after an hour but still edible within these times!

I hope your date is as easy as that!

Sautéed Vegetables

(fried basically!)

It's widely accepted that your meat should be accompanied by two vegetables. If you manage to get one away, I think we'll be doing well.

Broadly, there are two types of veg – those that you cook by boiling or steaming them and those that you cook by sautéing them. Once you know how to boil, steam or sauté one vegetable, you know how to do them all. The trick is to know which to steam and which to sauté.

As discussed in the *Remedial Tips* in the Sautéed Potatoes section, sautéing basically means frying and tossing something about in a saucepan. Although there are quite a few vegetables that can be sautéed, the only ones worth eating are mushrooms and onions.

The technique is to slice the onions or mushrooms thinly enough that they cook through quickly. Just be careful not to cut them too thin – aim for a little fatter than the thickness of the mushrooms and onions on a good pizza.

Next comes the substance in which to fry them. Some suggest butter, some suggest oil. I find that a little of both works best. Butter tends to burn at a lower temperature but if you use oil as well it won't.

Next thing to bear in mind is the heat at which to fry them. The pan mustn't be too hot or everything will burn. If it's too cold your veg will just get soggy. Make sure the pan is preheated to a medium heat – that's 3 on the 5 notch scale.

Next is to watch your timing – these things only take a couple of minutes to cook so there's no point in cooking them an hour before the meat is ready – do these last. Now you're ready to sauté.

The Recipe

• Toss all of the onions or mushrooms (or both) into the pan. Let them cook for a minute before you start poking them about. Now (technically) you should toss these about without the use of a spatula but I recommend that you cheat – adopt a hybrid, sauté/stir-fry approach.

• After about 3 minutes they should be done.

• Toss them out onto some kitchen towel to absorb all the excess grease, sprinkle a little salt and pepper over them and serve them up straightaway.

Cheating Tip

Mushrooms and microwaves go very well together – simply place the sliced mushrooms in a bowl. Drizzle a little olive oil over them. Sprinkle them with salt and pepper. Stick them in the microwave on full power for 1 to 2 minutes. Hey presto – non-sautéed, sautéed mushrooms!

Steamed Vegetables

(even sounds healthy, doesn't it?)

Now, you'll note that I dropped the idea of boiling vegetables. There are two reasons for this. One genuine reason and one that's true but too boring to consider as a motivating factor.

The real reason is that boiled vegetables can be ruined very easily by overdoing them – they turn into limp, tasteless bits of rabbit food. It's unlikely that you'll time your starters, meat, potatoes and vegetables perfectly so I want to make sure that you have as much leeway as possible. In this regard, steaming is far more forgiving. The second reason is that steamed vegetables are better for you because they retain more nutrients (boring but true).

For those of you who are still in the dark about this technique, steaming involves cooking your food in a piece of apparatus known as a 'steamer' – basically where one pot with a lid on top and holes in the bottom, sits over another pot, which contains boiling water. The steam penetrates the holes, thus cooking the food.

The cooking process is simple from here and involves you cutting your chosen vegetables into the desired shapes. I favour a bit of creativity here. While there is very little you can do with mange-touts or broccoli, there is plenty you can do with a carrot, a parsnip or a turnip. A serving of carrot cut into symmetrical blocks is a million times more appealing than a serving of the circular discs your date is used to.

Once you've settled on your veg, and you've chopped them into the desired shape, simply allow them to steam for the following durations. The water in the steamer should be boiling in normal Jacuzzi-like fashion and remember, your veg will remain tasty and edible even if you leave them steaming for way longer.

Vegetable	How many minutes to steam for?
Carrots	15–20
Turnip	20–25
Parsnip	15–20
Mange-tout	10–12
Broccoli	10–12
Peas	8–10
Cabbage	12–15

Once you're ready to serve up, simply toss the cooked veg into a (nice) serving dish. The general consensus suggests that you should put a knob of butter over the vegetables, which melts and delivers a rich flavour. That's fine, but please don't do it if I'm your guest cos I think it tastes too buttery, thanks.

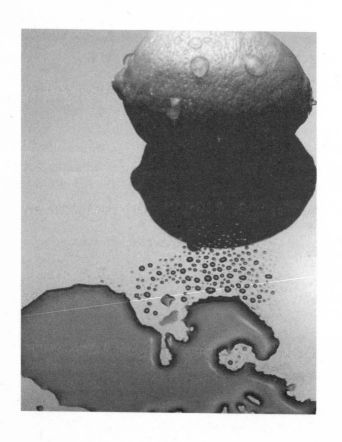

CHAPTER 4

INTER COURSES

I just couldn't resist! Despite the fact that there is only one recipe that fits this section, I just had to include it for the chapter title alone … Inter courses, intercourse, tee hee hee!

Yep, the only course you can possibly serve between other courses is, in fact, sorbet (pronounced 'sore-bay'). And the funny thing is that you'll never use it. Complete waste of time. Far too much work, and whoever you serve it to is simply going to look at you with that face that says 'SORBET???' They won't be impressed; they'll just be confused. Sorbet is something that most people only ever see served at a posh wedding and that's the risk you take – the Freudian message is marriage. Stop reading now and move on to the next chapter. Enjoy the title with this one and skip the next few pages!

Sorbet

Arabic, loose translation –
'oh, my God, they want to marry me'

INGREDIENTS

How much	Of what	Where to find them
4oz	sugar	In the press where you keep the coffee
½ pint	water	Guess!
½ pint	champagne	Cheat! Use a bottle that says 'sparkling wine'
Some	lemon juice	From a lemon
2	egg whites	From an egg

So you didn't heed the advice then? Your chances of getting lucky are diminishing by the second. As soon as you produce the sorbet your guest will start getting itchy feet. They'll simply think you're trying too hard. Mind you, for a small percentage of readers the message will actually be well received and the sorbet may actually pay ... or not.

To give this minnow of a meal the slightest chance of producing a result we need to employ our old friend, Mr Alcohol. And not any old rubbish, the big guns are needed here so we're going to wow your prey with some 'Champagne Sorbet'. It's a long shot but who knows? Your guest might have one of the following thoughts:

A: Sorbet ... SORBET? ... Bloody sorb, ... sorry, did you say *champagne* sorbet ... oh ... ooohh, you dirty devil, you're trying to get me drunk, fair play!

B: Champagne sorbet – I knew you had style as soon as I clapped eyes on you. You my friend have just scored 10/10 – GTOQ – get them off quick.

Remedial Tips

Sorbet is the closest you're ever going to get to eating a snowball – that's what it looks and feels like. Mind you, it should taste an awful lot better given the quality of the ingredients that make it up.

Posh people use sorbet as a palate cleanser between meals, i.e. it gets rid of the taste of the last course – a bit daft especially if they really liked the taste. Anyway, its fresh, crisp taste coupled with the acidic properties of the lemon juice help to leave your gob nice and clean so that the taste of the next course isn't compromised. Load of old tosh if you ask me.

Where Most People go Wrong

The fact that you're actually trying to make this stuff means that you've already gone wrong. Trust me, cut your losses now. If you're absolutely determined to serve up a sorbet, I'd have more respect if you'd at least cheat. Don't bother with the instructions below – just mush up the yellow part of a Loop the Loop ice-cream and serve.

Still reading? Boy, you're determined. OK loser, lets get this over with.

The Recipe

- Start by heating the water over a medium heat. Actually forget that, put the sugar in a saucepan, boil the kettle and throw in half a pint on top of the sugar.
- Put the pan on a medium heat and boil until the sugar is completely dissolved.
- Allow the pan to cool slightly and throw in the champagne and lemon juice.
- Allow to cool completely, and then put it in a glass bowl in the freezer and leave it there for 2 hours. The mixture needs to be semi-frozen. Fully frozen is ok, fully liquid isn't.
- In the meantime whisk the egg whites until they're stiff.
- When the 2 hours are up, take out the mixture and 'fold' in the egg white – basically this means do it slowly, don't beat the crap out of it!
- Stick it back in the freezer until it assumes an ice-cream like texture.

Now all you do is scoop it out into a nice glass and watch the look on your date's face. If they (and I bet they will) glance down at the plate then look up at you, then at the plate again and then back at you with a 'what the hell is going on' face, try to pass it off as some form of joke. A comment like 'you're so hot I thought you'd better have something to cool down' might work. In hindsight it probably needs to be a lot funnier and sharper than that! Good luck (you need it).

Variations

We know God loves a tryer, but even he would be encouraging you to give up at this stage. If you insist on having an inter course but can't stretch to the champagne version here are a few variations that may tickle your fancy. I stress the word 'your' because the likelihood of them tickling your date's fancy is similar to the likelihood of finding a wo-man who owns just one pair of shoes or a man who could talk to Pamela Anderson while looking her in the eye.

Lemon Sorbet
Here you need to add the juice and the pared rind of 3 lemons to the sugar/water stage. Follow the recipe through as normal, leaving out the champagne.

Orange Sorbet
As above, but use the juice and rind of 2 oranges.

Raspberry Sorbet
Here you need to mix the lemon juice per the original recipe with a pound of raspberries and a measure of kirsch (a fruit brandy – leave it out if you have none, or replace it with any fruit brandy/liqueur that you do have).

The next stage is a bit homemade. Purée the lemon juice, kirsch and the raspberries. You'll be left with something that resembles runny jam, and full of bits. To get the bits out you need to pass the mixture through a nylon sieve. Yes, I know you don't have one so get a pair of your or your sister's cleanest tights and strain the liquid through that instead – I'm not joking. When the SAS are bunked out in the desert, this is exactly what they would do when they realise they left the nylon sieve at home.

Carry on through the recipe replacing the champagne with the raspberry juice stuff.

CHAPTER 5

BREASTS AND BEEF (AND A BIT OF FISH)

So, when buying meat, chicken or whatever, there's usually a very good reason why two seemingly identical pieces of meat might have an amazing price difference. And when you're on the dating circuit, you need to splash out an extra bit to give your meal every chance of culminating in a bit of lovin'.

So to help you justify the expense here are a few reasons for the extra cost.

Beef

For those of you who don't already know it, the term beef refers to cows generally. So when you're in your local fast food emporium (rural term for a take-away) and you see a sign that says 'all our burgers are made from 100% beef' this really means '100% cow'. In case I need to spell it out, this means any part of the cow can appear in your burger – eyes, ears, tongue, bum, nose or whatever. The spinal chord is the only bit that escapes the mincing machine. Now are you getting a feel for why one would pay more for specific bits of the cow?

Another myth with beef is that fresh meat is better than well-hung meat. Contrary to what your dirty little mind is saying, well-hung meat refers to the length of time that the meat has matured and not the length of the meat itself. If you want to drag this train of thought down even further consider the fact that, technically, your dad is better hung than you are (whether you're a bloke or a girl!).

Well-hung meat tends to be far more tender than fresher meat. You can usually tell well-hung meat by its colour.

Ironically it's the stuff that looks less appealing because it has a darker colour and it even looks tougher. Because of this punters tend not to pick these less desirable lumps of flesh, so they'll probably stand out. If in doubt, ask the butcher. If you're feeling confident enough to proceed with the purchase yourself, take heed of the following guide.

Cut	Cost	What it Tastes Like
RUMP STEAK	If they're giving it away for free it's still too expensive	Like the handle of your dad's briefcase
ROUND STEAK	Should be really cheap	Like the sleeve of your brother's black leather bomber jacket
SIRLOIN STEAK	Dear enough to make your eyebrows raise	Lovely
STRIPLOIN STEAK	Dearer than the Sirloin	Gorgeous
FILLET STEAK	Dear enough for you to consider dropping your drug dealership and start dealing fillets	Yes, yes, yeeeessss

Chicken

The only bits of a chicken that I've used in any of these recipes are the breast fillets (the ones with no skin and no bones). Now not a lot of people know this, but the length of time that elapses between when a chicken hatches from the egg to the time it appears as two nicely sized breasts in your supermarket can be as little as 33 days (no that's not a typo).

The poor little geezers are kept in a well lit environment and basically sit there eating for a month. Free-range chickens, on the other hand at least have a decent and somewhat longer life before they meet you in the supermarket. This explains why they are far more expensive, but trust me, their cushy life al fresco is reflected in a far nicer taste too. Buy the more expensive ones. Your date will also approve of your humanity while tucking into Chucky the Chicken.

Fish

Fish is generally cheaper than meat but, as always, the ones that are harder to catch are usually the tastier ones and are always far more expensive than you expect. With fish it's just far easier to ask for help when you're buying it.

Chicken Parcels

INGREDIENTS

How much	Of what	Where to find them
2	chicken breasts	Meat counter – don't forget to get the free range ones
12	mushrooms	In the vegetable aisle – look for the white yolks that look like the things the Smurfs lived in
1	medium onion	Close to the mushrooms
1	red pepper	I'm insulting your intelligence now
Some	tinfoil	Down that aisle that you've never been down – the really boring one with the cleaning stuff and toilet rolls

The thing that I love about chicken is that it's just so hard to overcook it enough that your meal becomes inedible. If you boiled a chicken breast for an hour longer than you should have it might break up but you'd still be able to eat whatever you found in the saucepan.

This concept is very important – if you get lucky after the starter, you need to be comfortable knowing that your main course is flexible enough to survive overcooking while your sexual appetite is being fed. This is where the old Chicken Parcels work a treat. You could get laid, have a quick forty winks and still present your date with a fairly top notch piece of grub despite the fact that they'd have been cooking an hour longer than you expected. Depending on their gender, your guest will be thinking one of two things:

Male Guest: Chicken Breasts – oh I love breasts. Obviously a Freudian suggestion that she wants me to see hers. God aren't women great. And she can cook. Oh yes.

Female Guest: Chicken Breasts – obviously a Freudian intimation that he wants to see mine. God all blokes are the same. Mind you those parcels are to die for.

Remedial Tips

Mushrooms are a fungus and if they were any bigger they'd be scarier than spiders. They lack chlorophyll (sounds familiar doesn't it – the hamster in your head is racing round that wheel trying to remember what chlorophyll does), the green pigment that most plants use to make food. This doesn't bother our fungus friends. These guys live on dead plants and animals. If they weren't so nice to eat they'd be disgusting (eh … ah who cares if that's the most ridiculous comment ever – have you ever written a book smart ass?).

When shopping for mushies you're probably best sticking with the common-or-garden field mushroom. These are dead easy to spot in the shop. If there happens to be more than one type of mushroom available, the field mushroom is the one in abundance.

Where Most People go Wrong

Seriously, you have to be completely thick to muck this up. If you *are* thick, you're likely mistake is to pierce a hole in the bottom of the tinfoil parcel – this lets out the juices that will keep your chicken nice and juicy while you're otherwise engaged. Other than that there is no way you can get this meal wrong.

Ready? Let's go there, Delia.

The Recipe

• Preheat the oven to 160°C.

• Tear off two 12 inch squares of tinfoil. Lay them out side by side.

• Slice all of the onions, mushies and the pepper. Think of the style of the onions, mushrooms and peppers you get on your pizza – that's the style you want to be aiming for.

• Place a bed of the raw veg mix in the middle of each tinfoil square. Plonk a chicken breast on top and put some more veg on top of that. Don't worry if you think you've over done it with the veg. The more the merrier.

• Now simply make a parcel out of it. Any style you like. I tend to prefer the Dick Whittington style of parcel myself. If you don't get a mental picture of what I'm thinking about straight away just scrunch all the corners together.

- Bung it in the oven for at least 40 minutes and Bob's your uncle.

For a real lazy and foolproof accompaniment, chuck in a couple of baked potatoes at the same time.

When serving, simply open the parcel, pour out the juices and pour the contents out onto a (preheated) plate. Alternatively serve the baked potato with the unopened parcel for that extra air of anticipation. There's something strangely satisfying about opening a meal – it's like opening a present.

Yep, that took all of 5 minutes to prepare – if you don't get lucky, well at least you didn't waste much of your time.

Paella

Pronounced 'pie-el-ah' (in a Spanish accent)

Don't flick to the next page and be put off by the number of ingredients – this has got to be one of the easiest main courses ever. You have to hand it to the Spaniards – whoever thought up this meal must have been one lazy bastard. The beauty of this dish is that it looks the business.

You can prepare it in advance and finish it off in front of your guest or, even better, your mother can prepare it in advance and you can finish it off in front of your guest. It's an all in one job – most people cock up the main course by having their timing all wrong (you know, having the meat ready to go and then remembering to take the peas out of the freezer). That can't happen here. All of the meat, veg, etc. is in the same pot. You even save on the washing-up.

Once you plonk the pie-el-ah down in front of your guest, one of two things will be going through their mind:

A. Spanish food, what cultured tastes. This deserves a Spanish Kiss (like a French one but further south).
B. Moo-choose-grassy-ass you culinary God – you're getting lucky tonight.

You'll win either way.

INGREDIENTS

How much	Of what	Where to find them
2	cloves of garlic	Somewhere near the onions
3	vine tomatoes	The ones on the green stalks
1 medium sized	onion	If you've just found the tomatoes you should be close
¾ pint	long grain rice	Usually in the same aisle as the Pot Noodle
1½ pints	vegetable stock	Easiest to use stock cubes; your mum will definitely have these
¼ pint	white wine	Ask the bloke in the off-licence for the smallest and cheapest bottle he has
10 strands	saffron	Don't bother even looking, just ask
Some	fish	Go to the fish counter, tell them what you're making and ask them for a small piece of monkfish and a small piece of cod cut into bite-size chunks. Also get 2 scallops and about 10 tiger prawns
1	chicken breast	While you're getting your fish ask your butcher mate to slice up one for you
1	sauté pan (a deep frying pan)	You need to borrow one of these – preferably one with a lid. You'll be serving the pie-el-ah in this so borrow your mother's as it will be cleaner than any of your mates' pans

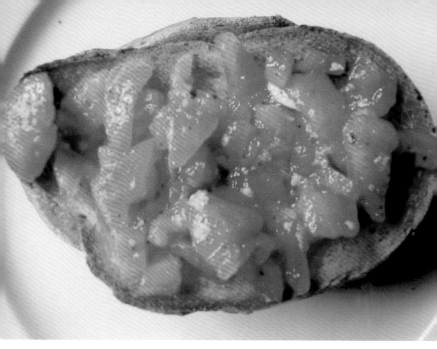

Bruschetta – don't forget the pronunciation, 'Broos-ketta'

Tortilla Chips with Tomato Salsa – pure fraudulence

Melony Prawn Cocktail, featuring two plates and a glass bowl

Smoked Salmon Wraps – can you believe this qualifies as cooking?

Sautéed Potatoes – warning, can cause heart attacks,
so you could taste and visit heaven in one go!

Paella: this one's made with a tub of fish bites

Lasagne (this one had a hard day at the office)

Chicken Parcels (before they were cooked)

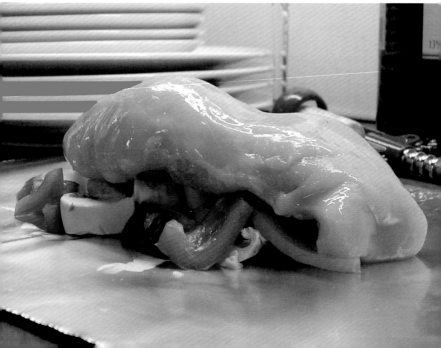

Bolognese, just add spaghetti
Sautéed Roast Chicken in a Brandy Pepper Sauce
(stop dribbling on the page)

Fillet Steak with Black Peppercorn Sauce (if you read the dedication
you'll understand why I cook this – a lot!)

Warm Chicken Caesar Salad – rabbit food it ain't

French Toast – the second-best invention by the French

Pancakes – hardest thing to cook in the book, honestly!

Cheesy Board, no cooking required

Banana Split – look, fruit, so it has to be good for you!

Remedial Tips

No, saffron isn't one of Bob Geldof's kids; it's a honey-scented spice. Being able to comment on its characteristics is always impressive, so here's a bluffer's guide. Saffron is a spice that comes from the crocus flower and, ounce for ounce, it actually costs more than gold. It does two things – it turns stuff yellow and gives it a flavour at the same time. You buy it in 'strands' and you'll be amazed how little you get for whatever you pay for it. You should throw in the following line at some stage over the evening for a few extra bluffer's points:

'My god, have you seen the price of saffron these days? It's so expensive. I'm thinking of harvesting some from the neighbours' crocus patch.'

Where Most People go Wrong

You absolutely can't go wrong if you follow the cardinal rule (which applies to any dish where rice is concerned):

DON'T STIR THE RICE – if you've ever wondered why your rice always turns out stodgy it's because you've stirred it. Stirring breaks the rice and releases the starch thus turning your lovely fluffy rice into the type of sludgy crap inmates serve up in Strangeways, proving that it's criminal to stir rice.

The Recipe

Ready? Then follow these steps:

There are two stages to this meal. You can do all of stage one in advance. Stage two should only be done 30 minutes before you're going to actually eat. Your mere organisation may be enough to impress the pants/boxers off your date.

Stage 1

- Fry the sliced chicken breast in a little olive oil until cooked through (should take 4–5 minutes over a medium heat). Remove the cooked chicken for the moment.

- Dice the onion and bung it into the pan with a little olive oil. Crush or finely dice the garlic cloves, throw them in with the onion and stir fry for a couple of minutes over a medium heat.

- Chop up the tomatoes as small as possible and add these (including as much of the juices as possible) to the onions and garlic and turn the pan down to a low heat. Add the wine and the chicken and allow to simmer for 10 minutes.

- Add the stock and crumble in the saffron strands. Bring to the boil, then turn the heat down to low and allow to simmer for a further 5 minutes

Stage 2

At this stage you're left with the fish and the rice and a pan containing the results of Stage 1.

- Make sure the contents of the pan are still simmering and sprinkle in all of the rice – give the pan a little shake to make sure the rice isn't sitting like a sugarloaf mountain in the middle of the pan – DO NOT STIR IT.

- Add the fish, put on the lid and walk away. The fish will cook perfectly with the steam and heat. The rice will absorb all of the liquid and turn yellow at the same time. As the heat is relatively low, it should take about 15 to 20 minutes for the paella to absorb all of the liquid. As always, give a quick taste before serving.

That's it, seriously. To make things even easier, bring the whole pan to the table and let your date serve themselves. Sit back, enjoy the nosh and look forward to that Spanish Kiss which should be winging its way in your direction within the hour.

Lasagne

Pronounced 'Lass-anne-yah'
(flick your head back when pronouncing the
'anne' bit to accentuate the Italian influence)

Ah yes, who can resist a bit of auld lasagne – the Italian equivalent of sausage, beans and chips.

Did you know that lasagne was a dish concocted by an Italian soldier for his maiden the night before he left for battle? Apparently the meat represented him, the tomato sauce her, the layers of pasta representing the sheets of their bed and the white sauce representing … you can finish this off yourself because it's all made up, total rubbish. It actually comes from the Latin word *lasanum* meaning 'cooking pot'. But it's important, when cooking Italian, to sound all loved up and romantic so act the part. Even if your date discovers that you're lying through your pants they'll still appreciate your efforts.

Chances are that they'll be as gullible as you hope they are so they'll buy all of the rubbish that you spin them. As they're tucking in to your luscious lass-anne-yah they'll really be thinking:

A. I hope the clothes slip off as easy as that rubbish slips off the tongue.
B. Mooch-o bellissimo foodo – lets heado upo to bedo.

INGREDIENTS

How much	Of what	Where to find them
300 gm	lean mince beef	In the meat fridge, find the sausages and you'll be in the right vicinity
½ can	chopped tomatoes	Your instinct will be to look near the beans, but you'll actually find them near the pasta
1 medium	onion	Keep an eye out for an orange coloured net bag
6	mushrooms	If your grocer adopts the alphabetical approach to stocking, the mushrooms will be in between the lettuce and the onions
1	clove of garlic	They come in bulbs – depending on your age you'll recognise them as the things David Soul used in *Salem's Lot* or Shaggy used in *Scooby Doo* to fend off vampires
¼ pint	water	Eh, the tap?
⅛ pint	red wine	Whichever is cheapest
1 pkt	tomato soup	One of those soup in a cup packets will do just dandy
1 amount	white sauce	See Cheating Tips
6 sheets	lasagne pasta	In the same aisle as the spaghetti, the rice and the Italian customers

Cheating Tips

Lasagne actually has two sauces – the meat sauce and a white sauce. Now you can make the white sauce yourself but trust me you'd want to (a) be assured of some serious return on your time investment or (b) be catering for Johnny Depp or Keira Knightly before it actually makes sense to make this yourself.

If an A-lister *is* actually coming, then heat 50 gm butter in a saucepan, stir in 50 gm plain flour; add in 1 pint of milk and 2 tablespoons of Dijon mustard and keep stirring until you have a nice thick white sauce. The chances of this are quite slim because there are just too many places where your sauce can burn, turn into slop, turn into concrete or simply taste awful.

The remedy? Cheat of course. You'd want to have the skills of a master aromatherapist before you can spot a home made white sauce from a decent bought one, so buy one instead. (PS it comes in a jar and you'll find them some-where near the Chicken Tonite sauces. And don't forget to get rid of the jar once you're finished.)

Where Most People go Wrong

Lasagne has to be cooked in a lasagne dish and if you don't have the right sized dish then you're destined for failure. In this case you're cooking for two so there's little point in bor-rowing your mum's dish as that's the one she uses to cook for a complete family. Use that one and you'll find that your meat sauce barely covers the bottom. You need one that's small enough for you to do at least two layers of sauce and pasta. Here's where you have to call up on a little brain power – look at the amount of meat sauce, the amount of white sauce and the amount of pasta you have and compare it to the dish you have to put it in. The ideal dish is the one that will just about fit everything.

OK, let's do this (you need to feel a bit pumped when taking on a lasagne).

The Recipe

The first job is to make the meat sauce and trust me, no one makes it like me. No one who writes does anyway and that's because the use of a packet of soup would make most chefs shiver in disgust. But who cares – remember you're not cooking for Nigella Lawson or Gary Rhodes so nobody will spot the shortcut.

- In a deep saucepan lob in some olive oil (veg or sunflower oil – it doesn't really matter) and warm to a medium heat.

- Dice up the onion and garlic and bung them in. Fry them for a couple of minutes.

- Add in the mince and cook it till it's nice and brown.

- Chop the mushrooms until fairly small and chuck them in and continue to cook for a minute or two.

- Now for the controversial step! Empty the packet of tomato soup evenly over the saucepan and stir until everything is coated. This will probably result in all of the juices being soaked up and the dish will begin to look all dry – fear not, this is all intentional.

- Pour in the water and stir – it is starting to look kinda edible now.

- Add the tomatoes and the wine and bring the sauce to the boil. Turn the cooker down to the first notch and allow the sauce to simmer for 30–40 minutes.

- In the meantime turn the oven to 170°C.

The next bit is child's play in comparison:

- Spoon half of the meat sauce into the lasagne dish.

- Cover the sauce with the pasta – try to cover the meat sauce completely by breaking off bits of the pasta and filling the gaps in a jigsaw-like fashion.

- Now cover the pasta with the white sauce – just use enough to cover it, don't go overboard. You've probably bought a jar suitable for a family portion so there's no need to use the whole jar!

- Now repeat the last 3 steps again, layering up the lasagne until you've reached the top of the dish.

- Lob the lasagne into the oven. You've about 30 minutes to spoof your date into the bedroom – so start working!

Spaghetti Bolognese

Pronounced 'spag-bol' if you're a Volvo-driving stockbroker

There are two reasons to serve spaghetti bolognese at an intimate dinner party. The first is so that you can introduce my 'strip spelling' game. You see 'spaghetti' is one of those words that no one can spell properly. So what you have to do is to invite your guest to join a game of strip spelling, challenging them to spell 'spaghetti' (properly) for, say, an earring or a watch. When they get it wrong you then introduce the rule where you keep asking the questions until they spell the word right.

Here's a list of common words and phrases that most people misspell – a list long enough for you to end up with one stark naked person sitting opposite you:

Separate Accommodation
(seriously, 9 out of 10 get this wrong, try it)
Resuscitation
Pneumonia
Entrepreneur
Bourgeoisie

INGREDIENTS

How much	Of what	Where to find them
300 gm	lean mince beef	In the meat fridge
3 well chopped	vine tomatoes	In the fruit and veg section. The vine tomatoes are the ones still attached by the stalks
I finely diced	carrot	In the vegetable aisle (they're the long orange things that Bugs Bunny eats)
I large, diced	onion	Near Bugs' food
I finely chopped	celery stalk	Although you never ate it for your mum, you have to put it in this dish
I	clove garlic	They usually put all of the stuff that makes your breath stink together so they should be near the onions
6 finely sliced	button mushrooms	The small white mushrooms
2 finely chopped	slices of streaky bacon	The butcher sells them in singles so you can avoid wasting the other 4 you'd have left over if you bought a pack
¼ pint	white wine	As usual, just get the cheapest you can find
¼ pint	beef stock	Mix a stock cube and boiling water

If they don't want to play strip spelling, then at least you know where you stand early on in the night! But don't get upset because the second reason to serve spaghetti bolognese is equally as effective at achieving the naked result. You see no one, not even God, can eat spaghetti without splashing at least one dollop on their clothes which opens the door for you to drop the 'oh dear, we better take you up stairs and get those dirty clothes off you' line.

Your guest will be thinking one of two things:

A.   Imagine thinking I couldn't spell 'spaghetti' – fool. Mind you I didn't see that 'we better take those dirty clothes off you' line coming. Fair play.

B.   I didn't know there were 3 Gs in spaghetti – but eating nude, we'll be doin' that again.

Remedial Tips

Spaghetti Bolognese gets its name from the two component parts – the pasta, spaghetti, and the sauce, bolognese.

The real cooking involves the cooking of the bolognese sauce, the pasta is really incidental. It could easily be served with any type of pasta – tagliatelli to make it tagliatelli bolognese; penne to make penne bolognese; fusilli to make fusilli bolognese, etc. In the spag-bol theme the latter is know as 'fus-bol' – a favourite for the boys.

Where Most People go Wrong
Like any stew type recipe it's almost impossible to go wrong with this dish. It's more likely that you'll make a mess of the pasta than of the sauce. If you do mess up the sauce you'll probably make it too runny, i.e. the wine and the stock and the juice of the tomatoes will make the sauce too watery – if this is the case, simply pour some away!

The Recipe
The cooking time with this is about 20 minutes, i.e. it'll take 20 minutes of your time to cook it but it has to be left simmering for about a further 1½–2 hours afterwards. In fact you could make it a day beforehand and heat it up on the night.

- Start by heating some olive oil in a deep saucepan to a medium heat
- Add the onions, garlic (crushed or finely diced) and the bacon and fry for 1–2 minutes
- Add the mince and fry until brown
- Add the carrots, celery and mushrooms and continue to fry for 2/3 minutes
- Pour in the wine and allow to simmer for 5 minutes
- Finally stick in the tomatoes and the stock, bring to the boil, turn the heat down to the first notch, sprinkle in some black pepper and a good pinch of salt – walk away!
- Let the sauce simmer for at least 1½ hours – if you forgot about it and came back in 4 hours it would still be gorgeous but don't test this out!

Serve up the sauce on a plate of your chosen pasta. Use spaghetti as it's the only one guaranteed to drip on your date's clothes.

Sautéed Roast Chicken Breast in a Brandy Pepper Sauce

Sounds scary, doesn't it!

Oh, yeah *shef*, you're moving to the big time now. This is about as close to real cooking as this book gets. But don't worry, despite the fact that this sounds like a university standard dish, it's as easy as pie.

The beauty of this dish is that the mere name, coupled with your delivery of this culinary illusion, will elevate you to the 'you lying bastard/bitch, you didn't cook that' category. Once you prove that you actually did cook it you'll instantaneously become more desirable. Your date will be so keen not to let you slip through their fingers that they'll already be thinking of marriage. This will become apparent from the blatant line of questioning that will inevitably follow:

Questions from the boys: So tell me, do you understand the offside rule then? (Answer 'Yes' and he'll be on his knees in seconds.)
Questions from the girls: So how much did you say you earn?

INGREDIENTS

How much	Of what	Where to find them
2 ample	skinless chicken breasts	In the meat aisle – don't buy anything before reading the comments about Chucky the Chicken at the beginning of this chapter
½ pint	vegetable stock	Make it from a stock cube which you'll find in your own press beside that massive Saxa bottle containing a ten year supply of salt
I	measure brandy	Under the cobwebs in your granny's drinks cabinet
I heaped tsp	butter	Fridge
I tbsp	cracked peppercorns	Look for a small seasoning container that says 'whole black peppercorns'. I'll tell you how to crack them below
150 mls	cream	In the shop, beside the milk
Good dollop	rich soy sauce	If you don't already own some, 2 sachets from your local takeaway will do the job

Remedial Tips

While it may be quite easy to get locked on brandy, it's an awful lot harder to get locked on brandy sauce. This is because the alcohol in the brandy evaporates at really low temperatures so by the time it hits your plate it's harmless. Therefore don't try the sleazy 'I'll get them plastered without them knowing trick' by lacing your sauce with loads of brandy, cos it won't work.

Because the alcohol evaporates so quickly you'll notice that the brandy liquor thickens up really quickly so it's really important not to have your saucepan too hot. You need it hot enough for the liquid to sizzle when you pour it on but not much more.

Also with this sauce, it's not actually essential that you use brandy – whiskey will do just as well. If you do change the alcoholic base remember to change the name of the dish accordingly – 'Scotch Whiskey Pepper Sauce' or '25 Year Old Midleton Whiskey Pepper Sauce' or whatever.

As always, be discerning about the expense you go to. The Middleton should be saved for the Demi Moore/Colin Farrell calibre of guest.

Where Most People go Wrong

There are two elements to this dish – cooking the chicken and making the sauce – if it's going to go wrong you'll cock up the sauce.

When you're making the sauce there's really only one thing that you'll do wrong and that's by having the heat up too high. You will need to bring the sauce to the boil but this does not have to happen in seconds! A low heat will still bring stuff to the boil, it'll just take a little longer so have some patience.

So are you ready to enter the realms of pseudo cookery? Let's go so!

The Recipe

Step 1 – Cook the chicken
Now there are umpteen ways to cook a chicken breast and there are umpteen more ways to mess it up. Here's my guide to how you can do it and how it will go wrong:

How to cook it	*Where it'll go wrong*
Frying it	Burnt on the outside, raw on the inside
Boiling it	It'll look anaemic
Roasting it	It'll be too dry
Grilling it	It'll be too dry and too burnt
Steaming it	It'll look even more anaemic than its boiled cousin
Deep frying it	It'll will develop bullet proof skin that you won't be able to cut through

Trust me – I speak from experience! The only way to cook a chicken breast so that (a) it looks good (b) it's actually cooked right through and (c) it's still nice and juicy, is as follows:

• Heat the oven to 160°C and boil the kettle (to make your stock).

- Put a little olive oil in the pan and heat to a medium heat (3 on the five-notch scale)

- Place your chicken breasts in the pan and walk away for about 3 minutes.

- Return and flip them over – the cooked side should be nice and brown. Leave them for another 3 minutes to brown on this side.

- Take the breasts off the heat and put them in a small ovenproof casserole dish. At this stage they look lovely but I guarantee you that they're completely raw on the inside.

- Make and pour the vegetable stock over the breasts so that they're just half covered and bung them in the oven – walk away.

The breasts will be cooked perfectly in about 25 minutes but the beauty of this approach is that no matter how long you leave them in the oven, they'll still be juicy. Once the stock doesn't evaporate you'll get away with overcooking them for up to an hour.

This gives you plenty of time to get the sauce right.

Step 2 – Make the sauce

Now, there are two ways to make the sauce – either in the pan you fried, no sorry, sautéed the chicken in, or in a new clean pan. Technically the dirty pan is actually better and gives a more flavoursome result. But don't worry, you can start off with a nice clean saucepan and still get the 'you liar, you didn't cook that' reaction.

- Turn the pan on to a low heat – say 2 on the five-notch scale.

- Once the pan has heated up, pour on the brandy and stir it into the crusty remnants that the chicken has left behind – this is called deglazing the pan. The brandy should be sizzling and will evaporate quickly. Don't be afraid to take the pan off the heat to control the temperature.

- Once the brandy has reduced by half, i.e. half of it has disappeared into thin air, add in the butter. This should melt and start to sizzle straight away.

- Pour in the cracked peppercorns (bash the whole peppercorns with something hard to crack them! Alternatively use a pepper mill)

- Stir this mixture around for approx. 30 seconds and then pour in the cream.

- Now all you have to do is bring the cream to the boil – slowly.

- Once it's simmering (bubbling slowly) add in the soy sauce – as well as enhancing the taste, the soy sauce gives the sauce an orgasmic colour and now it should be looking like someone proficient cooked it.

- Allow the sauce to simmer for 2 minutes or so and you should notice that it starts to thicken up. Turn off the pan now.

- If your timing is mucked up and the chicken isn't ready, don't worry, the sauce can be reheated.

- Now pour a few tablespoons of the sauce over each chicken breast. This goes really well with sauté mushrooms and sauté potatoes.

Sit back, enjoy the grub, and watch out for the marriage speak to start as soon as their tongue stops licking the plate!

CHAPTER 6

SURE BETS

Warm Chicken Caesar Salad with Crispy Bacon
Medallions of Fillet Steak with
Cracked Black Peppercorn Sauce

Rest assured that there are always a couple of meals that have global appeal and therefore are sure to impress any guest at your table. There are two reasons why this will benefit you. Firstly, as soon your guest hears what's on the menu there will be a palpable easing of the tension in the air simply because they will be so relieved that the dish is something they actually like. Secondly, the quality of the dish that you serve up will be far greater than any they've paid for in a restaurant. Trust me, there are a couple of ways to ensure this.

Having given them one of their favourite dishes, cooked to perfection, you might as well get up from the table, start undressing and tell your guest that you'll be waiting for them upstairs. Yes they'll think that you're being presumptuous but they'll also be thinking that they need to play their cards right if they're going to secure this quality of sustenance going forward. A bit of a poker play but worth it if they fold.

Warm Chicken Caesar Salad with Crispy Bacon

Jeez, I think my own pants have just fallen off

INGREDIENTS

How much	Of what	Where to find them
I head	lettuce	Free ones can be found in any neighbour's greenhouse
20	seedless black grapes	Hidden and almost impossible to find amongst the seeded ones
2	chicken breasts	The ones you want are the pricey ones beside the cheap battery chicken breasts
I lump	parmesan cheese	Near the easy-singles – like a block of cheddar except its white and probably cut into a slice
4 slices	streaky bacon	In a vacuum pack near the sausages
2 portions	caesar sauce	See *Cheating Tips*

Don't be put off by the side of you that's thinking of rabbit food – this dish will convert the most ardent carnivore into the healthy way. Anyway, it's not actually that healthy – rich dressing and lovely fatty bacon, ooops there go the pants again.

And that is the same reaction your guest will hopefully have unless you've been very discerning with your choice of guest and they are already going commando. Once your guest claps eyes on this dish they'll be thinking one of two things:

Normal guest:	Wow, chicken Caesar with crispy bacon – Did my pants just fall off?
Commando guest:	Wow, chicken Caesar with crispy bacon – I think my bottom just fell off.

Remedial Tips
Lettuce comes in loads of different guises. The type that Bugs Bunny eats (the one that looks like a huge green rose) is the Butterhead lettuce. The stuff that comes on your Big Mac is Iceberg lettuce and the one that should be served in your Caesar salad should be Cos lettuce – with big long crispy leaves. If you can't get a head of Cos, use either of the other two types.

Cheating Tips
To make a homemade Caesar sauce you need to get out your notebook, alert the deli and get ready to have your heart broken because this is the biggest pain in the ass exercise ever, in the whole world, ever ever. Caesar sauce is made of the following: garlic, eggs, lemon juice, Worchester

sauce, olive oil, parmesan cheese, wine vinegar and bloody anchovies, that's right, anchovies.

I'm not even going to bother telling you how to mix this up to make the sauce, there's no point – the chances are it will only taste a fraction as nice as the sauce that's sitting in a bottle beside the mayonnaise screaming 'buy me, buy me, I'll get you laid, buy me'.

Nobody considers the use of a bought Caesar sauce as cheating and the beauty is that it's absolutely taboo for a guest to question if the sauce is homemade or bought. So what you need to do is pour the bottle of sauce into a glass mixing bowl, and leave a whisk in it. Inevitably you'll be asked for more sauce and it will quash any doubts that it's homemade when you produce the bowl saying, 'I'm so glad that it's not going to waste, a lotta love went into that sauce'.

As regards which one to buy, look for one from the company representing the original Caesar Cardini – an American bloke who concocted it in the 1920s. Alternatively, look for one made by an actor who gives all his profits to charity, if such a thing exists.

Ready? Come on so Julius ...

The Recipe
There are a couple of stages to this meal – the preparation of the salad and the preparation of the meat.

Chicken

First job is to cook the chicken breasts – as someone who hates repeating myself (that's right, I can't stand repeating myself), you need to flick back to the Sautéed Roast Chicken Breast in Brandy Pepper Sauce recipe. You see the bit entitled 'Step 1 – Cook the chicken'? Yeah, follow that.

You need to pay a bit of attention to your timing here, but only a bit. It's important that the chicken is 'warm' when you stick it on your salad. So bear this in mind. If you happen to get sidetracked upstairs, on the couch, on the stairs or wherever, you can always use a microwave.

Bacon

For the bacon you need to be a bit more hands-on. Crisping up a few slices of bacon is simple but you need to keep a close eye because you want it crisp without being burnt. So here's how to do it.

• Fire up the grill until it's fairly hot – (turn the knob to 4 on the five-notch scale)

• When it's hot stick on the bacon

• Leave it cooking for about 2 minutes and then keep turning every 40 or 50 seconds until they become very well done (but not burnt). They should also become firm. That's right, the limpness will disappear and be replaced with viagra bacon. If you hold one end they should stand up straight.

• Now it's done, take it off, set aside and read on. (Unlike the chicken, the bacon doesn't need to be warm when serving).

Salad!
You're on easy street now.

- The first job is to wash your hands because you need to tear the leaves of lettuce into small pieces – aim for one-inch squares.
- Slice the grapes in half
- Using a potato peeler, peel off loads of the Parmesan cheese.

Now it's a simple case of building the salad:

- Place a bed of lettuce on a large dinner plate – a good portion, but don't overdo it
- Scatter half of the grapes on top
- Now drizzle some sauce over the salad in a zigzag fashion – again don't overdo it. If they want more they can ask (and this will give you a chance to produce the glass bowl with the homemade looking sauce in it)
- Scatter a good helping of cheese on top.
- Now carefully place two slices of bacon in an X shape on top
- Finally, slice the chicken breast and reassemble it on top of the bacon.

Serve up, sit back and keep an ear out for the faint sound of pants, boxers, thongs, g-strings or y-fronts hitting the floor.

Medallions of Fillet Steak with Cracked Black Peppercorn Sauce

Followed by a Barry White album for dessert

INGREDIENTS

How much	Of what	Where to find them
2 x 8oz	fillet steaks	At the butcher's counter. If the shopkeeper is wearing an apron covered in blood you're in the right type of shop
1 measure	brandy	Look for the bottle that says Cognac
1 heaped tsp	butter	Same place you keep the milk
1 tbsp	cracked peppercorns	Un-cracked ones will probably be in your peppermill. Using your peppermill will crack them
150 mls	cream	In the shop, beside the milk
Good dollop	rich soy sauce	If you have to buy some try and find one that's 'distilled' or rich

For women, the only thing that tops this meal is a brand new handbag and a pair of boots.

For blokes, a six-pack, free house and a Merseyside derby will just pip it.

This meal is sublime, and the trick to serving one that's better than any you've had in a restaurant is to pick the right bit of meat to cook first. If you're in the area go to Dessie Conway in Dalkey. If not, follow this guide.

The tenderness is largely dictated by the age of the meat. Contrary to popular belief, if you went out, shot Daisy the cow and cut a fresh fillet there and then, it's likely to be as tough as nails. Meat that has been hanging for a while is far superior. The well-hung stuff is not that appetising to look at when raw – in fact you'd probably avoid it like the plague if you didn't know better. It will have a deep red colour and the edges will be almost purple. The edges may also look crusty or completely gone off.

I'm not joking. Steak fitting that description will melt in your mouth when cooked.

And when it's set out on a plate in front of your guest (male or female) they'll only be thinking one thing – 'after all these years IT IS the quality of the meat NOT the quantity'.

Remedial Tips
Medallions of beef bear no resemblance to the medallions that appear around the necks of manly men. Medallions for culinary purposes are basically fat strips of steak. So job

number one is to cut the fillet steak into medallions – aim for lumps about the size of a Milky Way bar.

Where Most People go Wrong
There are two elements to this meal – cooking the meat and making the sauce. You won't go wrong. (Secretly I've hypnotised you so you won't go wrong. Did you get that? You won't go wrong. You are a strong powerful *shef* who won't cock up).

However, you might forget to cook something to go with your fillet steak. This is where you'll ruin your meal. Aim for something simple where you can manipulate your timing. Baked potatoes give you 15–30 minutes leeway. Mushrooms can be zapped in two minutes in a microwave. If you put a bit of thought into it, you won't go wrong. You won't go wrong. And if you ever meet the author, you'll give him €20, you'll give the author €20.

The Recipe
• First thing to do is heat the oven just to keep things warm later – 100°C will do nicely.

• Next heat a little olive oil in a frying pan – medium heat (3 on the five-notch scale)

• When the pan is hot, start frying the medallions. Once you place them on the pan for the first time, leave them alone. Don't feel under pressure to keep poking them about. The trick to cooking medallions of fillet steak to perfection is to only turn them once. You should let them fry for about 3–4 minutes before turning them. You might find that the medallions develop a Toblerone type shape –

i.e. that they have three sides, so you'll actually be turning them twice.

- When all sides have been exposed to the heat for their 3–4 minute frying session, take them off and place them on a plate in the oven, and turn the pan down to the first notch (for the sauce).

Now we want to make the sauce. Funnily enough, even though I've given the sauce a brand new name, it's actually the same sauce that we used for the Sautéed Roast Chicken Breast in Brandy Pepper Sauce in Chapter 5. What a conman! So, through the magic of cut and paste, here's what to do:

- Make sure the pan is still hot (should be on the first notch), pour on the brandy and stir it into the crusty remnants that the ~~chicken~~ medallions have left behind – this is called deglazing the pan. The brandy should be sizzling and will evaporate quickly. Don't be afraid to take the pan off the heat to control the temperature.

- Once the brandy has reduced by half, i.e. half of it has disappeared into thin air, add in the butter. This should melt and start to sizzle straight away.

- Pour in the cracked peppercorns (bash the whole peppercorns with something hard to crack them! Alternatively use a pepper mill)

- Stir this mixture around for a few seconds – 30 approx – and now pour in the cream.

- Now all you have to do is bring the cream to the boil – slowly.

- Once it's simmering (bubbling slowly) add in the soy sauce – as well as enhancing the taste, the soy sauce gives the sauce an orgasmic colour and now it should be looking like someone proficient cooked it.

- Allow the sauce to simmer for 2 minutes or so – and you should notice that it starts to thicken up. Turn off the pan now.

Now simply arrange the medallions on warm plates and pour over the sauce. *Voila*!

You'll note that I haven't got all uptight about how well done the meat is – rare vs well done, etc. The timing above will be sufficient to cook the meat to perfection – beautifully tender and just the slightest hint of pink in the middle. If your guest makes any comment about the doneness of the meat (other than to say it's perfect) – slap them across the face and take away their medallions as punishment. They won't make the same mistake again.

In fact try slapping them anyway to see if that glint appears in their eye – you now the one that says 'naughty, naughty'. If that doesn't appear, just say 'missed him the little bugger' and start to dart your eyes around looking for a fly.

CHAPTER 7

DESSERTS

Chocolate Sauce
Ice-cream with Chocolate Sauce
Banana Split
Baked Alaska
Cheesy Board

At this stage of the evening your guest should be so impressed with the starter and main course that the sexual innuendo is already evident in the conversation – 'whoever gets you will be very lucky ... blah blah', etc. If the food isn't the source of the flirting then the wine that you've been plying them with should be taking effect. Wine-based flirting is usually a bit more honest – 'is it my imagination or is it hot in here? Can I take off your clothes? That'd be cool!'

If, however, they're still playing hard to get then these few recipes will sort them out. No one can get through one of my desserts without some ooohhhing and aaahhhhing. When this starts, simply glance at them knowingly. My desserts are orgasmic so what you're hearing is a trailer for the real thing.

Chocolate Sauce

INGREDIENTS

How much	Of what	Where to find them
100g	milk chocolate	Irrespective of which brand you buy, it'll be in a bluey/purpley wrapper next to the Mars Bars
150 ml	cream	Beside the milk

The aim here is to finish off the leftover sauce by having your date lick it off you. Given that this sauce is simply the highest quality chocolate substance you will ever taste, your objective is eminently achievable. From here on in you will be eating it for breakfast, it's that good. And what's more, it's the simplest recipe in the book. If you get this wrong, give up, go home.

Your date will be contemplating two things:

A: If they're trying to get me into bed I think they've just succeeded.

B: Oh look I've just fallen into the chocolate sauce; do you want to lick it off?

Remedial Tips

Cream is sort of like milk but thicker. When it comes to buying it for this dish you can buy pouring cream or double cream. Double cream is thicker and therefore your date runs a slightly higher risk of cardiac arrest – at least they'll die happy.

Where Most People go Wrong

As I said, if you get this wrong, give up. Seriously, piss off.

The Recipe

Ready to get saucy?

- OK, get a pot and pour in the cream

- Break in the chocolate

- Turn the ring to full and wait a minute until you see little bubbles appearing around the circumference of the cream. This means it's almost ready to boil – don't let it, (if you do, don't worry).

- Take the pot off the heat and stir until the chocolate is fully melted.

That's it! Now pour it over your guest and tuck in.

Alternatively use it as an accompaniment to one of the following recipes.

Ice-cream with Chocolate Sauce

If you think I'm going to give you a recipe for ice-cream I think that you've missed the objective of the book, which (for those of you in the 'I don't know what you mean' category) is not to cook if at all possible. That's right, don't cook if you can avoid it AND definitely don't cook something that's not going to taste anywhere near as good as something you'd buy. Ice-cream encapsulates the very essence of this rule, so there.

So buy some ice-cream – vanilla will do nicely; scoop out a few nicely-formed balls of the stuff, stick 'em on a nice plate, lash on as much of the chocolate sauce as you're willing to part with and get ready to hear the culinary orgasm which will be along shortly. The real one should follow as a matter of course.

Banana Split

As per the Ice-cream with Chocolate Sauce recipe (above), however, for this one split a banana lengthways, put the ice-cream in between and pour the sauce over the top.

Baked Alaska

Ooooohhh- aaaaahhhhhh

INGREDIENTS

How much	Of what	Where to find them
100g	caster sugar	Your mum will have some of this and you'll probably find it beside the flour
2	egg whites	From 2 eggs
1	jam swiss-roll	Actually you can use any spongy type cake. Raid your mum's press – every old dear has a Madeira stashed away
½ block	vanilla ice-cream	Beside the Choc-ices. Use two Golly Bars if they've run out of blocks

Do you remember when Meg Ryan was doing her orgasm scene in *When Harry Met Sally*? This is exactly what will happen when your guest tastes this.

This dish defies belief. It's called Baked Alaska because you stick a block of ice-cream in the oven and it doesn't melt. And I'm not lying. And I'm not cheating – the oven *will* be on, and bloody hot.

You're going to elevate yourself to legendary status with your date. Even if you get dumped they'll always remember their magical dessert of ice-cream from the oven.

Remedial Tips

You're going to be making meringue (pronounced *merr-ang* not *mer-ing-gee*). Be prepared, this is actually real cooking. What you need to do is get the white part of the egg, i.e. the entire inside of an egg except the yellow bits. The easiest way to do this is to crack an egg into your (clean) hands and let the white bits drip into a bowl. If the yellow bit cracks chuck everything out and start again – you can't have any of the yolk in the egg white or this won't work.

Then you need to beat the living daylights out of it until it goes nice and fluffy. You'll need to borrow a mixer for this. When the egg whites get reasonably stiff (little peaks will hold their shape) you need to mix in the sugar. Keep the mixer running and add in the sugar, bit by bit. The merr-ang should get really stiff and look glossy. Dip your finger in and taste – delish eh! You shouldn't really eat this raw (salmonella and all that) but it's really hard to resist.

Anyway, merr-ang has a really unusual property and that is that it is one of the best insulators known to man. It laughs in the face of fibreglass and lagging jackets. So when you cover your block of ice-cream with it, it insulates it perfectly from the heat and it doesn't melt. I've never even met you and I almost want you at this stage. Imagine what your date will think.

Where Most People go Wrong

Unfortunately there are loads of places to cock this dish up, so pay attention. These are the major stumbling points:

- Mixing in the tiniest bit of egg yolk will mean that your egg whites will never stiffen.

- If you don't have enough meringue covering the ice-cream its insulating powers will be diminished and your ice-cream will melt.

- If you forget about it and leave it in for too long, the meringue will burn and your ice-cream will melt.

Feeling up to this, Delia?

The Recipe

OK – I'm assuming that you've made the meringue per the *Remedial Tips*, so the rest of the job is mere assembly. Start by firing up the oven to 180°C.

- Place your spongy type cake on an oven proof plate – large enough to take a fat coating of meringue. The base of the sponge should be slightly larger in size than the ice-cream.

- Next, place the well-frozen block of ice-cream on top.

- As quickly as possible slap on the meringue, making sure that you cover every part. Your ice-cream is now well insulated.

- Pop it in the oven.

Now you need to keep an eye on this because some ovens seem to operate on a turbo basis and others on a Honda 50 basis. Leave it in for at least 8 minutes but keep checking. The meringue will go a fawn type colour when it's done.

Don't worry if you take it out a little early, it'll still be gorgeous. The inside of the meringue will be really light and fluffy, while the ice-cream will be as hard as concrete (well not quite but you get the point).

Serve and wait for the Meg Ryan impression.

Cheesy Board

INGREDIENTS

How much	Of what	Where to find them
12	crackers	As variety is the spice of life, buy three different packets and have a range on display.
12	green grapes	Go to the off-licence, look at the picture on the label of any bottle of wine. The fruit on the front is a grape. Green ones can be found in the fruit and veg section (of the supermarket dopey, not the offey)
12	black grapes	Beside the green ones above. Make sure they're seedless by the way
Some	cheese	See *Remedial Tips*

Ah yes, the Samson and Delilah dish. Picture the scene. You on one side of the table, your left elbow in the middle of the table, you're draped forward, leaning to the left, your head in your upturned palm. Your date is mirroring you on the opposite side, open mouthed as you ram grapes and gorgonzola down their neck. Ding-dong. Is that wedding bells I hear?

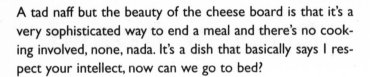

A tad naff but the beauty of the cheese board is that it's a very sophisticated way to end a meal and there's no cooking involved, none, nada. It's a dish that basically says I respect your intellect, now can we go to bed?

Remedial Tips
Although cheese comes from milk, it doesn't have to be cows' milk. So you can get goats' cheese, cows' cheese and sheep's cheese. Theoretically you could make cheese from any animal that produces enough milk for you to harvest. Somehow I don't think that pig cheese or cat cheese would be that appealing but who knows.

In addition to easi-singles, cheese also comes in many other guises – soft mouldy ones, soft fresh ones, hard ones, smoked, blue and washed versions. For your cheese board you'll need to visit your supermarket to see what's on offer. Buy one for yourself that you know you'll eat and three or four others to make you look worldly.

You might find that there are pick and mix selections of individual portions – these are perfect, as you don't need to waste copious amounts of cash on large lumps of mouldy cheese that will go in the bin as soon as your date leaves.

Where Most People go Wrong
Other than your date referring to an allergy to dairy products, there is no other way to mess up here. Unless of course you're completely thick and you went for the easi-singles and Calvita wedges.

The Recipe

OK there? If you've ever been called cheesy, now is your time to shine.

Wash (and dry) the grapes and arrange them, the cheese and the crackers on a board (or plate) in a manner pleasing to the eye.

Wasn't that easy? Now start ramming them down your date's neck in a *9½ Weeks* fashion. (And for the younger readers, *9½ Weeks* was Kim Bassinger's first big flick featuring Mickey Rourke and the luckiest ice-cube ever made.)

CHAPTER 8

COCKTAILS

Between the Sheets
Flaming B52
Morning Glory
Kamikaze
Dizzy Blonde
P.S. I Love You
Kir Royale
Black Russian

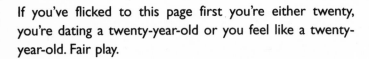
If you've flicked to this page first you're either twenty, you're dating a twenty-year-old or you feel like a twenty-year-old. Fair play.

Here's the scene.

It's 8.24 p.m. You said half seven for eight. The main course will be edible until about 11 but you were aiming for 9.30. You've checked to make sure the phone isn't off the hook (twice). There's a ring at the door ...

You	Hi, Come on in (in a 'the price is right' type of way).
Them	Oh, smells lovely.
You	Me or the dinner, *(nervous laughter – tee-hee-hee).* What will you have? Wine? Tea? Long Island Iced Tea? Me? A Slow Comfortable Screw Against the Wall?
Them	Oh, cocktails?
You	No, I actually meant a slow comfor ... only joking.
Them	What would you recommend?
You	Do you trust me?
Them	As if.
You	Good, knock this back so and say goodbye to your 'no sex before marriage' aspirations.

Unfortunately I can't condone the use of alcohol to get your wicked way. (Apparently all is not fair in love and war). Seriously, drink sensibly. You can let your guest look after themselves.

As regards this section I have assumed that, although you know nothing about cooking, you do know everything about drinking. The necessity for *remedial tips* explaining where to find Pernod is superfluous. Also, you'll note that the only directions with these recipes are to mix them together. Even if you cock that up, the mixture will still be alcoholic and drinkable. Therefore I've dispensed with the *where most people go wrong* section as well.

When serving cocktails there are definitely those that appeal to the boys and those that appeal to the girls. Blokes' cocktails will usually have loads of alcohol, no mixers and can be knocked back in one go. And if you can set fire to it, it's definitely one for the boys.

Girly drinks are usually nicely coloured and have a bunch of accessories attached – umbrellas, handbags, shoes and stuff. The real giveaway of a lady's cocktail is the name – Pink Lady, Dizzy Blonde, Shirley Temple, Natter Natter, Lovely Shoes, etc. Oh, and finally, most of them have champagne in them.

For the Boys

Between the Sheets

Need I say more? Sometimes the name says it all. Serve up one of these and you won't even make it to the starters before the sloppy wet kisses and the octopus hands come out!

What you'll need (for 2):
1 measure Brandy
1 measure Bacardi
1 measure Cointreau
Juice from half a lemon
Ice

Shake everything in a cocktail shaker – this basically cools the drink down to freezing without having to actually serve the ice in it – leave the ice behind when serving. Split the cocktail between two glasses. This is a fast-acting beverage – it's more likely you'll get between the cushions of the couch rather than actually between the sheets but that hardly matters.

Flaming B52

How to turn on your bloke instantaneously lesson no. 1 – serve up one of these, saying: 'you look like the sort of guy who, when you go down, you'd like to go down in flames.' Watch out for the hands diving into the pockets to re-arrange the involuntary activity!

What you'll need (for 2):
1 measure Baileys
1 measure Kahlua
1 measure Cointreau
Ice

You can shake this in a cocktail shaker but if you're going for the B52 flambé you'll need to layer the liqueurs by pouring them slowly into the glass. If you pour them in the correct order, they should separate into distinct layers; the right order is Baileys, Kahlua, Cointreau. The Cointreau can be torched but be careful – if it burns too long, the rim of the glass will heat up so much that your lips will stick to it when you take a sip. Be warned!

Morning Glory
Now some of you ladies may not know this, but the term 'morning glory' refers to the erectness of a man's bits when they wake up – no kidding, and yes that *is* what Oasis are singing about. As these go down, the morning glory will arrive prematurely!

What you'll need (for 2):
1 measure Brandy
1 measure Orange Curacao
Dash of Angostura bitters
Dash of Pernod
Ice

Using the shaker, mix all of the ingredients together. Leave the ice behind when you're pouring it out. On the inebriated scale he'll be giggling after one, telling you secrets after two, dribbling after three and proposing after four.

Kamikaze

Similar to the Flaming B52, the Kamikaze allows a variation of the 'bet you love to go down in flames' innuendo. However this time the innuendo is a bit more menacing and dominatrix-esque. What you do is serve it up saying 'this is a Kamikaze. I thought it might suit because I bet if you were hit you'd go down'. A dazed rabbit look followed by an enormous gulp will follow. You've scared the pants off him but, being a bloke, he's game and he'll stand his ground.

What you'll need (for 2):

1 measure Vodka
1 measure Cointreau
1 measure lime juice or lemon juice
1 measure lemon cordial
Ice

As usual, shake all the ingredients in a shaker and pour out, leaving the ice behind. When he knocks back the first mouthful of this cocktail, he'll be hit by the overpowering lemon taste which will make him wince like he would when he's ... you know ... enjoying himself, so to speak. Take note because you could be staring at that expression at close quarters later.

For the Girls

Dizzy Blonde

Did you know that blondes are a dying breed? Seriously. You see blonde girls attract blonde blokes. BUT fake blonde girls also attract real blonde blokes, resulting in diluted blonde kids. Eventually real blondes will be wiped out and replaced by some mongrel variation. This should suit me because I think that mousy brown may become the new blonde.

Anyway, my recommendation to you is for you to tailor the name of this drink to suit your girl. No woman is going to like the connotations of a 'dizzy blonde' irrespective of her own hair colour. So capitalise – if your date is a four-foot redhead with green eyes, call the drink an Angel Eyed Devil Head Cherub – get the drift?

What you'll need (for 2):
2 measures Advocaat
1 measure Pernod
Lemonade
Ice

Do not shake this in a shaker – the fizz from the lemonade will pressurise and blow the shaker (and your expensive booze) asunder. Simply pour the Advocaat and the Pernod into two glasses, add some ice and top up with the lemonade. After a couple of these you'll be dating a dizzy blonde, dizzy redhead, dizzy brunette, dizzy skinhead or whatever.

P.S. I Love You

This drink came out before the *P.S. I Love You* book in case you're wondering! As with the Dizzy Blonde, you might also want to change the name of this drink; P.S. I Love You may scare them off. Call it a P.S. I Fancy the Pants off You or a P.S. I Think your Legs have a Lovely Curvy Top on Them, or something along these lines.

What you'll need (for 2):

1 measure Amaretto
1 measure Tia Maria or Kahlua
1 measure Baileys
Ice

Simply pour all of the ingredients into a couple of glasses and proceed to pour the glasses into your date. After one, she'll be flushed, after two she'll be telling you why you're so much better than all of the other losers she's dated and after three she'll be telling you that this drink should be called a P.S. Take me to Bed.

Kir Royale

If you've ever bought one of these in a public bar you already know what's in it because you would have fainted when you got the bill – the expense coming from the fact that it's made of champagne and red stuff. Anyway, you're on home territory now and you can aim for some economies of scale – you need to buy a bottle of champers so you might as well use the lot. And you know what they say about champagne mixed with females? Champagne makes girls dance and drop their pants – apparently this is a well-known side effect so beware if Auntie Mary asks for one.

What you'll need (for 2):
Dash of Crème de Cassis
Champagne

Simply put a dash of Crème de Cassis in the bottom of a champagne glass and top it off with champers. 'Cook' for about 20 minutes and wait for the oncoming signs of dancing: 'do you have any Abba', etc. You know what's coming next!

Black Russian

The only genderless cocktail in my opinion – one for the boys and the girls! And its best property is that it's the most palatable cocktail of the lot. And the best thing about being palatable is that they'll drink it more quickly. And the best thing about that is that the emphasis will be taken away from your cooking so you can serve up any old slop. In addition, her beer goggles will be on so you might get lucky into the bargain.

What you'll need (for 2):
1 measure Vodka
1 measure Tia Maria or Kahlua
Coke (the soft drink, not the drug)
Guinness
Ice

All you need to do is split the ice, Vodka and Kahlua between two glasses and top up with coke. If you happen to have a can of Guinness handy, pop in a half measure into each glass and stir (gently) – this gives a lovely head. Ironically your own head will not be so lovely the following morning.

CHAPTER 9

THE MORNING AFTER

Pancakes
Omelettes
French Toast

Breakfast Recipes and Quickies
Meals you can serve up in minutes

If you're here for some genuine help with cooking brekkie, then presumably last night got a result. Well done. The fact that you're bothering to serve up something other than cornflakes and toast suggests that this could be serious. Should I nip out and book a tux?

It's important that you produce these breakfast dishes nonchalantly — you don't want it to appear that the breakfast was premeditated. In reality, that's exactly what it is, so you need to make sure that you've an ample supply of bread, milk, eggs, flour and sugar — for some reason most breakfast dishes only use these ingredients.

These recipes may appear substantial. This is intentional, as you'll need to keep your stamina up.

Pancakes

(for those of you who like a bit of crumpet)

INGREDIENTS

How much	Of what	Where to find them
2	eggs	Although you keep them in your fridge, the shopkeeper keeps them somewhere near the fruit and veg
4 heaped tbsp	flour	Plain, self-raising, or whatever you can find in your mum's press
3 heaped tbsp	sugar	In the same press as the coffee and the hobnobs – am I right?
½ pint	milk	Find a cow and tug frantically on the bits sticking out underneath

'Oh, what'll I do for breakfast? All I have is eggs, flour, sugar and jam. Eh … emmm … eehh … eeeeeee … Oh I know, I'll do some pancakes.' You're such a fraud!

Remedial Tips and Recipe
As this is fairly involved, consider this recipe one big long remedial tip!

This isn't the easiest thing in the book – in fact it's one of the hardest to master. But, like riding a bike (or riding generally) once you've done it right once you'll never forget how to do it. My advice is to whip up a bunch in advance if trying this for the first time.

The first thing to do is to put the flour and the sugar into a bowl, stir them around and make a well in the middle into which you crack both of the eggs.

Now the following technique is very, very important. Mix the eggs into the flour by gradually taking flour from the side, i.e. concentrate the mixing in the centre of the bowl and the liquid egg will attract and stick to small amounts of the sugar and flour. This technique will ensure that you minimise/eliminate the amount of lumps. At the end of this process you'll end up with a fairly thick batter that'll almost be too thick to mix.

Now gradually pour in the milk and keep mixing. The end product should be similar in texture to cream soup. You might need more than the half pint of milk that I've budgeted – don't be frightened, whatever mixture you end up with, too runny or too thick, it'll still turn out edible.

Next you need to heat your non-stick frying pan (did I mention this?). Yes, a non-stick pan is absolutely essential for making pancakes. Anything else and you'll end up with your pancakes welded to the base of the pan.

You need to heat a small amount of oil to an almost medium heat – what this means is put the pan on a ring turned to 3 on the five-notch scale. Once it's hot, switch it back to 2.

Now pour in enough mixture to cover the base. I'm talking about a thin layer here, not a deep puddle of pancake mix. The actual amount that you will need to cover the base depends wholly on the size of your pan. I prefer a small pan but only because they're easier to turn over.

Leave the pancake to cook for about two minutes. Now for the hard part – turning it. Your options are (1) toss them à la Gary Rhodes or (2) carefully flip them with a spatula – your call!

Allow it to cook on the other side for a minute or two and simply turn it out onto a decent plate, as you'll be serving it up on this.

And the serving suggestions are endless – you can fold them, roll them, leave them flat, carve out initials on them or even cut out two eyes and a mouth and wear it as a mask. Oh the fun.

Omelettes

INGREDIENTS

How much	Of what	Where to find them
2	eggs	In the pockets of any protestor outside government buildings
Some	milk	In the carton labelled 'milk'
2 slices	cooked ham	From a cooked pig

So how *do* you like your eggs in the morning? In a 'girly magazine' fashion, pick your favourite answer and see below for a scientific commentary of your personality:

A. Unfertilised
B. I like my eggs with a kiss
C. I like my eggs like my men – hard on the outside, soft on the inside and easy to crack
D. I like my eggs beaten with milk and fried

And the results are:

If you chose (A) you're a bloke. You're probably in your late teens. You think Rachel Stevens is to die for and that Liam Gallagher would definitely take Robbie Williams. You're probably still laughing at the 'unfertilised' answer and you'll tell the joke all day long.

If you chose (B) you're most likely to be a girl but you could possibly be a bloke who is very much in tune with his feminine side. You're in the late twenties/early thirties bracket; you're single but have had a string of brief relationships with guys who laughed at your Westlife and Robbie Rat Pack albums. You recognise the 'I like my eggs with a kiss' lyric as Helen O'Connell's response to Dean Martin's question. You're a lovely person. Really.

If you chose (C) you're definitely a woman, with a job, a real job and a VW Golf. You firmly believe that blokes need to be trained and you persistently brush off advances by all blokes, even those you actually want. The brush off is on the basis that if they are worthy they'll keep trying. You're probably really good looking and other women hate you. Mike Skinner wrote a song about your type but you still don't recognise the association.

If you chose (D) you love omelettes. You are fantastic. You are well endowed; your bum doesn't look big in that; women want you, men want to be you; have you lost a few pounds? Where did you get that handbag and those shoes are to die for.

Remedial Tips

Omelettes bear a remarkable resemblance to scrambled egg. In fact in my house they are identical apart from the fact that you stir your scrambled eggs while cooking them – the omelette is poured into the pan and left to cook, pancake style. Yes, an omelette is basically a flat scrambled egg dish – unscrambled eggs if you like.

Where Most People go Wrong

The temptation to flip an omelette in the same fashion as you'd do with a pancake is almost irresistible. Trust me, you don't want to do this.

The Recipe

OK, first things first. This recipe is enough for one omelette. They're fairly filling but if you're feeling piggish, sorry, peckish, simply cook two!

- Crack the eggs into a bowl and add some milk. I say 'some' because it doesn't really matter if you add a dash or a ¼ pint – you'll still get an omelette. It's just that the one with more milk will be lighter and fluffier than the other. So pour in the desired amount of milk and mix up well.

- Add some salt and pepper.

- Chop up the ham and throw it in.

- Now heat some oil in the pan to a 'just below' medium heat, i.e. turn the pan to 3 on the five-notch scale and once it's hot turn it back to 2. The omelette shouldn't cook instantaneously – the coolness of the liquid should take the heat out of the pan nicely.

- Now, while the omelette is cooking slowly, turn on the grill to about 4 (on the five-notch scale). Rather than flipping the omelette, you can cook the face up side by sticking it under the grill (leave it in the pan when grilling).

- Judge its doneness by looking. If you get a burning smell you're useless.

Now toddle back to bed and deliver those eggs that have been the cornerstone of your line of chat for years.

French Toast

French Toast – definitely the subject of one of those mystical questions – you know the ones:

• Do they sterilise the needle before administering the lethal injection?

• If you were in your car travelling at the speed of light and you flicked on your headlights, would they work?

• If salting the road gets rid of ice how come icebergs don't dissolve in the sea?

• In France do they ask for Toast or French Toast?

Ooohh la la. Stroke your chin when you propose these questions back in the bedroom to make it appear that you're deeper than you really are.

Remedial Tips

Eggs come from chickens. Or, more accurately, chicken eggs come from chickens. Now there are a few things that you need to know here, as your level of humanity will dictate how much you pay for them. Nowadays every Irish egg has a code stamped on it denoting whether the egg was laid by a free range chicken/an organic one or a chicken reared in poultry's equivalent of Alcatraz. Pay attention to the code and pay a little extra for the egg.

Where Most People go Wrong

As with any toast-making situation you need to make sure that you don't burn your French Toast. Pay attention to the heat of the pan when you start cooking – a medium heat is what you need (that's 3 on the five-notch scale).

The Recipe

• OK, start by beating the eggs with some salt and pepper and about an egg-cup full of milk.

• Pour the mixture out onto a plate. Plonk a slice of bread on top and let it soak up as much of the mixture as it'll hold. Turn it over to make sure that both sides have absorbed their full quotient.

• On your pan heat a little oil to a medium heat. Place the bread in the centre and allow it to cook on this side for about 3 minutes. Flip it over and let the other side cook – a nice brown patchy look denotes a well-cooked slice.

• Repeat for slice 2.

Off you pop back to the bedroom stroking your chin with your French toast and your (Irish) coffee. Don't forget the whiskey.

Index